institutions. Throughout, **Can Capitalism Survive?** is a masterful array of essays – penetrating, witty, and wise prescriptions for our day.

Benjamin A. Rogge is Distinguished Professor of Political Economy at Wabash College, in Crawfordsville, Indiana. He cautions us not

to overinterpret that title, describing it as "what they hand out at small colleges to senior faculty members in lieu of cash." He has been at Wabash since 1949, serving variously as a teacher of economics, academic dean, and director of the Wabash Institute for Personal Development (an executive development program based on the liberal arts). His articles have appeared in both professional and general-circulation publications. **Introduction to Economics,** a college-level textbook, was written in partnership with his longtime department superior, John V. Van Sickle. Rogge holds degrees from Hastings College (A.B.), the University of Nebraska (M.A.), and Northwestern University (Ph.D.). His professional memberships include the American Economic Association and the Mont Pelerin Society. In politics, in common with one of his intellectual mentors, F. A. Hayek, he identifies himself as an Old Whig.

Can Capitalism Survive?

Can Capitalism Survive?

Benjamin A. Rogge

LibertyPress
Indianapolis

Liberty*Press* is a publishing imprint of Liberty Fund, Inc., a foundation established to encourage study of the ideal of a society of free and responsible individuals.

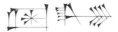

The cuneiform inscription that serves as the design motif for our endpapers is the earliest known written appearance of the word "freedom" (*ama-gi*), or liberty. It is taken from a clay document written about 2300 B.C. in the Sumerian city-state of Lagash.

Library of Congress Cataloging in Publication Data

Rogge, Benjamin A.
Can capitalism survive?
Includes bibliographical references and index.
1. Capitalism—Addresses, essays, lectures. 2. Economics—Addresses, essays, lectures. 3. Laissez-faire—Addresses, essays, lectures. I. Title.
HB501.R674 330.12′2 78–17378
ISBN 0–913966–46–0

This volume is a publication of
the Principles of Freedom Committee

The great body of economic and political literature since World War II—both academic and popular—has presented a misleading picture of the performance of private enterprise and of the State in the economies of the free world. This literature exaggerates the defects of the one and the merits of the other. Freedom will remain in jeopardy unless the public gains a clearer picture of the workings of the free market and comes to realize that its greatest virtue is not its extraordinary capacity to produce widely diffused material benefits, important as this merit is, but its unique capacity to protect the great immaterial values of our Western heritage.

As a means of increasing the flow of literature that would correct the picture and strengthen the foundations of freedom, a group calling itself the Principles of Freedom Committee was formed during the early 1960s to promote a series of books dealing with important economic and political issues of the day. To assist in the international publication and distribution of the books, the Committee recruited an advisory group of scholars from sixteen countries. *Can Capitalism Survive?* is the ninth book in the Principles of Freedom Series.

The membership of the Committee has changed over the years through retirements and replacements by cooption. The original members were Professors Milton Friedman, F. A. Hayek, G. Warren Nutter, B. A. Rogge, and John V. Van Sickle, Executive Secretary; Ruth Sheldon Knowles, Project Coordinator; and Byron K. Trippet, Committee Member Ex-Officio. Dr.

Trippet retired in 1965 following his resignation as President of Wabash College. Professors Hayek and Nutter retired in 1968, and three new members were added: Gottfried Haberler, Galen L. Stone Professor of International Trade, Harvard University; F. A. Harper, President, Institute for Humane Studies; and Don Paarlberg, Hillenbrand Professor of Agricultural Economics, Purdue University. In 1970 Gottfried Dietze, Professor of Political Science at The Johns Hopkins University, joined the Committee, and Kenneth S. Templeton, Jr., assumed the duties of Executive Secretary from Dr. Van Sickle. In 1973 Professor Yale Brozen of The University of Chicago replaced Professor Friedman as a member of the Committee. Following the deaths of Drs. Harper and Van Sickle, Professor Arthur Kemp of Claremont Men's College and Dr. Arthur A. Shenfield of Windsor, England, joined the Committee in 1975.

The original Committee requested modest nonrecurring grants from a number of corporations and foundations. These donors receive copies of all books as they appear, and their help in promoting the distribution of the books is welcomed. The Institute for Humane Studies handles the funds received from the project's supporters and issues annual reports. Decisions as to authors, subjects, and acceptability of manuscripts rest exclusively with the Committee.

Earlier volumes in the Principles of Freedom Series are:

Great Myths of Economics (1968), by Don Paarlberg

The Strange World of Ivan Ivanov (1969), by G. Warren Nutter

Freedom in Jeopardy: The Tyranny of Idealism (1969), by John V. Van Sickle

The Genius of the West (1971), by Louis Rougier

The Regulated Consumer (1971), by Mary Bennett Peterson

The Conquest of Poverty (1973), by Henry Hazlitt

Union Power and the Public Interest (1973), by Emerson P. Schmidt

Economic Growth & Stability (1974), by Gottfried Haberler

Contents

Foreword

One of the signs of advancing age in the American college professor is a tendency for him to write less and publish more. This seeming paradox is easily explained by the phenomenon of *Collected Works*, that is, by what on television would be described as reruns. As in television, no great public outcry is needed to bring forth the reruns; a question from his wife, a polite suggestion from a colleague, and the cut-and-paste operation is under way.

I have put together here what I believe to be the best of the rather meager output of my professional career up to this point. For reasons (mostly financial) that always seemed adequate at the moment, I have been more of a speechmaker than a writer. Thus, you will find that many of the pieces in this collection are but speeches put down on paper.

I have edited the manuscripts, but only to make them more readable and to reduce duplication of ideas and phrasings. In most cases, I successfully resisted the temptation to erase those statements that, in the light of later knowledge, would cast doubt on my omniscience (for example, some moderate words in praise of Richard Nixon, written in May 1971). The papers are grouped in categories that make sense to me, but obviously some of the papers could as easily have been placed in other groupings.

Some of those holding the markers for my intellectual debts are identified in the papers; others, just literally too numerous to mention, will have to be content with an occasional and probably very accurate, "But of course I said that long ago—and more elegantly."

Very explicit words of appreciation need be directed to Catherine Fertig, my secretary and an expert at deciphering handwritten manuscripts; to Marise Melson, my daughter and copyeditor, who is possessed of a good sense of style in manuscripts and in life; and to my late wife, Alice, for her patient, loving, and low-key nagging of me to finish this project.

Can Capitalism Survive?

Part I

Can Capitalism Survive?

The basic ideas of this paper were expressed on a number of occasions and in various forms. It was first presented in the exotic setting of a business conference held at the Playboy Club in Lake Geneva, Wisconsin. In somewhat different form, it was later presented in the Ludwig von Mises Lecture Series at Hillsdale College. I am presenting it here as the first paper because it poses the Big Questions—as identified by Joseph Schumpeter and agreed to by Ben Rogge.

Chapter 1

Can Capitalism Survive?

Can capitalism survive? No, I do not think it can. The thesis I shall endeavor to establish is that the actual and prospective performance of the capitalist system is such as to negative the idea of its breaking down under the weight of economic failure, but that its very success undermines the social institutions which protect it, and inevitably creates conditions in which it will not be able to live and which strongly point to socialism as the heir apparent.[1]

These words were written in 1942 by Joseph Schumpeter, Austrian-born Harvard social scientist, in his prophetic work, *Capitalism, Socialism and Democracy*. Inasmuch as I intend to build my comments around this work, it might be appropriate for me to reinforce my own judgment of Schumpeter's competence with a statement by the Nobel Prize-winning economist, Paul Samuelson. In one of his *Newsweek* columns in 1970, Samuelson wrote:

---

[1] Joseph A. Schumpeter, *Capitalism, Socialism, and Democracy*, 3rd ed. (New York: Harper & Row, 1962), p. 61.

> It is just twenty years since Joseph Schumpeter died. Although it is not my practice to tout profitable speculations, today I'd like to suggest that Schumpeter's diagnosis of the probable decay of capitalism deserves a new reading in our own time. The general reader cannot do better than begin with his 1942, *Capitalism, Socialism and Democracy*.
>
> Nothing that has happened in recent years at Berkeley or Harvard would come as a surprise to those who have absorbed this work. And if there are good clubs in the great beyond, one can picture Schumpeter—an 87-year-old by this time, martini glass in hand—reading *The New York Review of Books* and chuckling with clinical amusement. Only his Viennese veneer keeps him from saying, "I told you so."[2]

(In common with his sometime colleague at Harvard, John Kenneth Galbraith, Schumpeter was possessed of a very healthy ego. He is reported to have remarked in his later years that, as a young man, he had had three ambitions: to become one of the world's greatest economists, one of the world's greatest horsemen, and one of the world's greatest lovers. He continued by saying that he was happy to report that he had succeeded in two of those ambitions. He did not identify which two.)

I

On what does Schumpeter base his forecast, and how does all this relate to the life and times of the

---

[2] Paul A. Samuelson, "Joseph Schumpeter," *Newsweek*, April 13, 1970, p. 75.

American businessman today? Bear with me; all will be revealed in due course. We begin with the analysis.

(1) The first question that Schumpeter seeks to answer is this: Has capitalism proved to be a successful economic system in the sense of producing over time continuing improvement in the economic well-being of the masses? His answer to this is an unequivocal and resounding, Yes! In his words, "The capitalist process, not by coincidence, but by virtue of its mechanism, progressively raises the standards of life of the masses."[3] "Queen Elizabeth owned silk stockings. The capitalist achievement does not typically consist in providing more silk stockings for queens but in bringing them within the reach of factory girls in return for steadily decreasing amounts of effort."[4]

I direct your attention to his phrase, "not by coincidence. . . ." Critics of capitalism usually argue that the economic performance under capitalism in England and the United States was not the *result* of capitalism but of a combination of fortuitous circumstances and wise governmental action to counteract capitalist excesses.

Schumpeter takes each of the "fortuitous circumstances" in turn and discards them as possible explanations of the capitalist track record. For example, the virgin land and other natural resources of the Amer-

---

[3] Schumpeter, *Capitalism,* p. 68.

[4] Ibid., p. 67.

ican continent were but "objective opportunities" waiting to be exploited by an efficient economic system —and capitalism was that system. I might add that some million or so Indians lived lives of severe economic privation on top of those self-same resources in an area where over 200 million now live lives of Galbraithian affluence.

In the same way the technological revolution of the last two hundred years has been not an historic accident but a predictable concomitant of the capitalist system. More on this later.

To the claim that capitalism's success was significantly produced by governmental corrections of capitalist excesses, he makes two replies. The first is that the track record (in terms of improvement in real wages) was just as good in the period of minimal state intervention and minimal trade union activity (1870–1914) as in later periods. The second is that most such interventions actually reduced the rate of improvement in economic well-being. For example, he argues that the unemployment figure was increased by the anticapitalist policies of the 1930s. He concludes: "We have now established a reasonable case to the effect that the observed behavior of output per head of population during the period of fullfledged capitalism was not an accident but may be held to measure roughly capitalist performance."[5]

[5] Ibid., p. 110.

(2) Schumpeter turns next to the question of whether there are any purely economic factors that would prejudice the chances of capitalism continuing to bring improvement in the economic well-being of the masses. In this section, he is answering the doomsayers of the thirties (including and particularly John Maynard Keynes) who saw in the depression evidence of a deeper malaise in the capitalist economy, in the form of a vanishing of the investment opportunity that had sparked the capitalist engine for so many decades.

His attacks here are centered upon an enemy that has largely disappeared by now, as the "stagnation thesis" which so captured our imagination in the thirties has been undone by the simple course of events. I'll spare you the details of the argument and report only one of the assumptions of the stagnationists: that, by the late 1930s, all of the great technological breakthroughs had been made, and the capitalist world from then on would be missing this great stimulus to private investment spending. This is an example of what the *New Yorker* refers to as the "clouded crystal ball." Schumpeter correctly labels this assumption of the stagnationists as nonsense and describes their other assumptions as either equally nonsensical or irrelevant. His conclusion is that there were no purely economic factors to obstruct continuing success for the capitalist system.

(3) In his answer to his next question, Schumpeter presents what I believe to be the most accurate and

useful description of the nature of competition under capitalism ever developed. His question is this: How can capitalism be so successful a system when capitalist reality has always been at such odds with the perfect competition requirement of the textbook models? There are only two possible explanations. One is that "fortuitous circumstances" produced economic growth in spite of the gross imperfections of the capitalist system—but Schumpeter has already denied the validity of this thesis. The second, and the one for which he opts, is that the traditional textbook model of competition and monopoly, with its emphasis on perfect competition as the ideal and the target, is simply not relevant. As he puts it, "If we economists were given less to wishful thinking and more to the observation of facts, doubts would immediately arise as to the realistic virtues of a theory that would have led us to expect a very different result."[6]

Perhaps the best way to explain the difference between the textbook and the Schumpeter models of competitive behavior is with an example. In Table A you are given the shares of the diuretic market held by various firms over a ten-year period. By the criteria of the textbook model, each year—taken separately—would reveal a grossly imperfect market structure. Why? Because a few firms dominate the market. In addition (although the data given here do not reveal

[6] Ibid., p. 75.

Table A

Drug Companies' Shares of the Diuretic Market, 1951–1960

Letter = company
Digit = trade name product

	A1	B2	C3	D4	F6	G8	G9	H10	H12	J13	Others
1951	32%	22%	19%	17%							10%
1952	9	25	37	18							11
1953		23	33	12	15%						17
1954		10	16	5	59						10
1955		6	13		61	13%					7
1956			11		67	9					13
1957			9		67		12%				12
1958					14			78%			8
1959					10			58	18%	7%	7
1960					8			45	23	7	17

Source: Marketing Division, Eli Lilly Company, Indianapolis, Indiana

this), the profit margins on these products for the leading firms each year would most probably be very handsome indeed—perhaps far above what would be thought to be a "normal" profit. The technical description of the market structure, in the language of the textbook model, would be that of "oligopoly"—the rule of the few.

All of this Schumpeter would label as nonsense. Why? Because the investigator would be examining "each year—taken separately" rather than the never-ending game of leapfrog that the data reveal and that represents the true nature of the competitive process.

To the textbook economist, both the size of the firms relative to the market and the high profits on individual products would be evidence of market imperfection, implying "corrective" action (e.g. breaking up the larger firms). To Schumpeter, not only are size and profits not anticompetitive per se; both are natural and desirable features of the competitive process, when viewed as a dynamic process operating through the course of time. The size is often needed to assure innovative efficiency, and the profits are needed to keep the challengers trying. (In fact, says Schumpeter, when the losses of the failures are combined with the profits of the successes, the net cost to the consumer of all this may be zero—or less.)

Neither the Yankees nor IBM nor General Motors need be dismembered; time and tide and "creative destruction" will operate on each and bring a demotion in rank—unless they behave as if they face immediate and equal rivals, i.e. unless they behave "competitively." And, of course, unless they receive governmental assistance in maintaining their market positions.

Schumpeter concludes his work in this area by saying that "long-run cases of pure monopoly must be of the rarest occurrence. . . . The power to exploit at pleasure a given pattern of demand . . . can under the conditions of intact capitalism hardly persist for a period long enough to matter . . . unless buttressed by public authority."[7]

My own conviction, deriving largely from Schumpeter, is that competition does not have to be created or protected; it inheres in the very nature of man. It can be reduced or eliminated *only* by coercive acts of governments. All that a government need do to encourage competition is not to get in its way.

I agree with Schumpeter's words in his preface to the second edition of *Capitalism, Socialism and Democracy,* when he writes, "I believe that *most* of the current talk about monopoly is nothing but radical ideology. . . ."

In my opinion the antitrust laws of this country are anticapitalist in intent and in effect and, in addition, constitute one of the major sources of confusion and unwarranted guilt feelings on the part of the businessman. These laws brand as antisocial precisely those

---

[7] Ibid., p. 99.

achievements by which the businessman evaluates his performance—growth in size, superiority over rivals, increasing market share, profits above average, etc.

They also produce such absurdities as the case brought a few years ago against Topps Chewing Gum for monopolizing the baseball picture card industry. In the words of the FTC examiner, Topps had been "hustling around getting the players' signatures, pretty well cornering the major league players." He added, in a dramatic after-climax, that "players were paid $5.00 for a five-year contract." Who could possibly compete with a company that was willing to throw money around like that? (That was ten years ago; today, under the influence of potential rivals, the figure has gone up to no less than $250 a year!)

(4) Schumpeter's case for capitalism is now complete and it is impressive indeed. Why does this not assure the public and political acceptance of the system? Because, says Schumpeter, "it is an error to believe that political attack arises primarily from grievance and that it can be turned by justification. . . . In no case is [rational argument] a match for the extra-rational determinants of conduct."[8]

In effect if capitalism is to survive, it must defend itself in the arena of values and emotions—and here its very success as an economic system reduces its chances of victory. We can best see Schumpeter's analysis of

[8] Ibid., p. 144.

this by examining the impact of capitalism on each of the groups in society that might serve as a bulwark against the system.

(5) We begin with the principal beneficiaries of capitalism—the masses. Why do they not defend the system that has made them the most affluent people in the history of man? Because they do not connect their affluence with the capitalist system, because they are incapable of understanding *any* economic system as such, because they are more aware of their daily frustrations and insecurities under the system than they are of their long-run gains from the system, and because they are taught by the intellectuals in society to resent the capitalist system and its central figure—the businessman.

This same point is eloquently made by another distinguished social observer, Ortega y Gasset. In *Revolt of the Masses*, he writes:

> The common man, finding himself in a world so excellent, technically and socially, believes it has been produced by nature, and never thinks of the personal efforts of highly endowed individuals which the creation of this new world presupposed. *Still less will he admit the notion that all these facilities still require the support of certain difficult human virtues, the least failure of which would cause the rapid disappearance of the whole magnificent edifice.*[9]

[9] Jose Ortega y Gasset, *Revolt of the Masses* (New York: Norton, 1932).

(6) The traditional aristocratic element in society that in the nineteenth century tended to protect the liberal capitalist system from its radical critics is itself a victim of the capitalist success. Capitalism is rationalistic in nature and creates an unfriendly climate for the tradition-based class system of the precapitalist society.

(7) But why does any of this matter? Can't the businessman be his own defender? Why must he rely on others? Why indeed. The response is that even if he were fully aware of the problem and determined to do something about it, the businessman lacks the capacity to capture the imagination of the society. In the words of Schumpeter,

> A genius in the business office may be, and often is, utterly unable outside of it to say boo to a goose—both in the drawing room and on the platform. Knowing this he wants to be left alone and to leave politics alone. . . . There is surely no trace of any mystic glamor about him which is what counts in the ruling of men. The stock exchange is a poor substitute for the Holy Grail.[10]

But this is not all. As capitalism matures, the form of the business firm and the role of the businessman change in such ways as to weaken the businessman's *will* to resist the critics of capitalism. Most importantly

---

[10] Schumpeter, *Capitalism*, pp. 138–9.

(to Schumpeter), with the growth of the large organization so essential to economic efficiency, the role of the individual entrepreneur is replaced by the work of the team, and innovation itself is reduced to routine. Personality is blotted out and with it the gut sense of ownership of the means of production that characterized the self-made man of early capitalism. Capitalism creates the organization man—and the organization man is indifferent to the fate of capitalism. He eventually comes to care little whether he reports to the anonymous stockholders or the anonymous citizen-owners of socialism.

A case in point from my own experience: As a college student, I was employed one summer by the privately owned gas distribution system in Hastings, Nebraska, to try to persuade the citizens of the city that it would be a most unwise action for them to vote *yes* on a referendum proposal for the city to take over that system. Each Monday morning we "customer relations" men were given an impassioned lecture by the manager of the system on the evils of socialism. In spite of our eloquence (or because of it), the good burghers voted four to one to take over the system. One week later the manager of the now socialized enterprise was appointed, and who was it? Old God-how-I-hate-socialism himself! (This illustrates a point I have long argued: the kind of aggressive, ambitious, effective person who succeeds under capitalism is also likely to rise to power under most other economic arrangements. It is only under capitalism that his drive is harnessed in service to the interests of the consumers.)

(8) The result of all this is to make of capitalism a virtually undefended fortress, but this alone would not mean its destruction. What is needed is an enemy force—and this too capitalism provides, in the form of the intellectuals.

How is the intellectual defined?

> Intellectuals are people who wield the power of the spoken and written word, and one of the touches that distinguishes them from other people who do the same is the absence of direct responsibility for practical affairs. . . . The critical attitude [arises] no less from the intellectual's situation as an onlooker—in most cases, also an outsider—than from the fact that his main chance of asserting himself lies in his actual or potential nuisance value.[11]

The intellectual tends always to be a critic of the system, of the establishment, whether he is in Russia or the U.S. In Russia he is not tolerated—or is attuned solely to serving the current rulers and their ideology. But the businessman is by nature tolerant. He wants to sell people something—not send them to Siberia.

The growing affluence of a mature capitalist society permits a continuing expansion in systems of higher education and hence in the ranks of the intellectuals. In fact, in 1942 Schumpeter accurately foresaw the

---

[11] Ibid., p. 147.

current surplus of intellectuals, surplus in the sense of there being far more intellectuals than employment opportunities with income and prestige equal to the self-evaluations of such people. For this, said Schumpeter, the intellectuals will hold the capitalist system responsible, which will add fuel to their already burning critical fires. Moreover, the widening gap between their own incomes and those of the businessmen will induce them to find ego-restoring explanations of the businessman's success—luck, exploitation, fraud, monopoly, etc. These rationalizations are described by Schumpeter as "the autotherapy of the unsuccessful."

One group that the intellectuals will seek to identify with and to stimulate to greater anticapitalist activity will be the workers. Schumpeter describes the advances of the intellectuals to them in words that would seem truly prophetic to anyone who has recently seen pictures of the adulatory groups around a Cesar Chavez. "Having no genuine authority and feeling always in danger of being unceremoniously told to mind his own business, he must flatter, promise and incite, nurse left wings and scowling minorities, sponsor doubtful or submarginal cases, appeal to fringe ends, profess himself ready to obey."[12]

A second group with which the intellectuals will feel a natural alliance will be the governmental bureaucrats, with whom they share a common educational back-

---

[12] Ibid., p. 154.

ground. In addition, of course, the bureaucrats will be increasingly involved in administering anticapitalist legislative policies. I might note that, to the intellectuals, these anticapitalist legislative creations will have a second happy feature—employment opportunities for themselves and their friends, carrying with them both decent pay and indecent amounts of power over others.

(9) The enemy and his allies are now at the gates of the capitalist fortress. Is there any hope that the businessman will finally sense the danger to himself and the system of which he is a part and rise to meet the challenge? As Schumpeter sees it, quite the contrary. Here are his words:

> Perhaps the most striking feature of the picture is the extent to which the bourgeoisie, besides educating its own enemies, allows itself in turn to be educated by them. It absorbs the slogans of current radicalism and seems quite willing to undergo a process of conversion to a creed hostile to its very existence. Haltingly and grudgingly it concedes in part the implications of that creed. This would be most astonishing and indeed very hard to explain were it not for the fact that the typical bourgeois is rapidly losing faith in his own creed.
>
> This is verified by the very characteristic manner in which particular capitalist interests and bourgeoisie as a whole behave when facing direct attack. They talk and plead—or hire people to do it for them; they snatch at every chance of compromise; they are ever ready to give in; they never put up a fight under the flag of their own ideals and interests—in this country there was no real

resistance anywhere against the imposition of crushing financial burdens during the last decade or against labor legislation incompatible with the effective management of industry. . . . Means of defense were not entirely lacking and history is full of examples of the success of small groups who, believing in their cause, were resolved to stand by their guns. The only explanation for the meekness we observe is that the bourgeois order no longer makes any sense to the bourgeoisie itself and that, when all is said and nothing is done, it does not really care.[13]

II

We now have in front of us Schumpeter's 1942 prediction of things to come—and a most unpleasing prospect it is indeed (at least to those who think even tolerably well of capitalism). What can we say of this prophecy in 1974? Is Schumpeter's analysis even now being validated by the course of events or is it not? I take no pleasure in reporting to you my own conviction that the course of events is lending ever greater credibility to the Schumpeter thesis. I do not propose to repeat here each piece of evidence that leads me to that conclusion. But here are some samples.

Do we or do we not have a surplus of intellectuals (as defined by Schumpeter)? Are they or are they not, by and large, critical of the American businessman and of the system of which he is a part? Do they or do they

[13] Ibid., p. 161.

not "nurse left wings and scowling minorities, sponsor doubtful or submarginal cases" (such as the lettuce boycott)? Do not these critics of capitalism largely control the world of the academy? of the media? of the pulpit? When did you last see a businessman treated sympathetically in a novel or a play? Whose name is better known to the American people: Ralph Nader or the president of General Motors or General Electric?

Can we find in the masses of the people any real understanding of the system that has heaped riches upon them or any instinct to defend from attack the central figure in that system, the businessman? Are they not, as Ortega has put it, the spoiled beneficiaries of a process they neither understand nor appreciate?

But neither of these would be of first importance if the businessman himself were even occasionally interested in the survival of the system, aware of what that really means, and willing to work for it. That he is not, in the typical case, any of these, most of the time, is more or less clear.

I offer in evidence the following examples: first, the tendency of the corporate leadership of this country to parrot the talk about the social responsibility of the businessman. With Adam Smith, I have never known much good done by a man who affected to trade for the public good. And, as Professor Milton Friedman has put it so many times, the way in which the businessman can *best* serve society is to try to maximize his profits within the law. Nothing is more clearly anticapitalist than the notion that the profit-directed activities of the businessman are antisocial, and the related notion that he can serve society only by eschewing that goal and directing his activities according to his (or some intellectual's) idea of the public good.

A second example is the response of the business community to the imposition of wage and price controls in the summer of 1971. For several years prior to that time, I had been collecting a folder of statements by leading businessmen demanding that such controls be established, and I have now added to that folder all of the statements from the same men (and their principal organizations) congratulating the President on his wisdom in imposing controls.

(It is of some interest to note that the first economist of note to congratulate President Nixon on his wisdom in imposing controls was John Kenneth Galbraith. Of course this compliment was a little backhanded; he noted that Nixon had opposed such controls throughout his political life but, as he put it, "fortunately the President is a man without principle or scruple, willing to do what is expedient and necessary." The fact is that Nixon took over a ship under heavy inflationary stress, induced by the unwise fiscal and monetary policies of his predecessors. It was as if the captain of the Titanic, immediately after his ship hit the iceberg, had turned to his second in command and said, "Now you've always wanted a ship of your own. Take over.")

Direct controls do not and cannot stop inflation (only an end to new-money-financed deficits can do that); they destroy the sensitive signal system that is at the center of a market economy; they are an economic absurdity and a moral monstrosity—yet we find them supported by some substantial part of the American business community. In fact, the response of the businessman to the general encroachment of government in his affairs has been similar to that predicted by Schumpeter and similar to the response of the native girl to Lord Jim's advances, described by Conrad as follows: "He would have ravished her, but for her timely compliance."

John Kenneth Galbraith and his friends have indeed taught the businessman well, and what they have taught him is to repeat the phrases that must eventually sound his own death knell. The capitalist fortress is indeed almost naked of defenders and is encompassed round with a host of enemies.

III

Are there no signs pointing in the other direction? Are there no bright spots anywhere? Must the Schumpeterian process work its way to its appointed end? Is there nothing that can be done? Is mine not a defeatist message?

I begin my reply with a statement by Schumpeter in the preface to the second edition:

> This leads to the charge of "defeatism." I deny entirely that this term is applicable to a piece of analysis. Defeatism

> denotes a certain psychic state that has meaning only in reference to action. Facts in themselves and inferences from them can never be defeatist or the opposite whatever that might be. The report that a given ship is sinking is not defeatist. Only the spirit in which this report is received can be defeatist: The crew can sit down and drink. But it can also rush to the pumps.[14]

As you would guess, I am suggesting that such as are inclined rush to the pumps. But is the situation really all that desperate? Are there any hopeful signs? The flow of human experience is always disturbed by eddies and cross currents and the cutting of new channels, and is always complex. There are *some* businessmen who are aware of and attempting to do something about the problem. Not *all* the intellectuals are critics of capitalism. But the flood tide is still close to what Schumpeter predicted it would be, and the outlook is anything but reassuring.

My self-assigned task here has been one of diagnosis, not prescription. I offer you in closing the only possible assurance of my presentation. It comes from that master student of human affairs, Adam Smith, and it was penned at a time when the outlook for capitalism was less bright than it is today. Here is what he had to say:

> This frugality and good conduct, however, is upon most occasions, it appears from experience, sufficient to com-

[14] Ibid., p. xi.

pensate, not only the private prodigality and misconduct of individuals, but the public extravagance of government. The uniform, constant, and uninterrupted effort of every man to better his condition, the principle from which public and national, as well as private opulence is originally derived, is frequently powerful enough to maintain the natural progress of things toward improvement, in spite both of the extravagance of government, and of the greatest errors of administration. Like the unknown principle of animal life, it frequently restores health and vigour to the constitution, in spite, not only of the disease, but of the absurd prescriptions of the doctor.[15]

[15] Adam Smith, *The Wealth of Nations* (New York: Modern Library, 1937), p. 326.

Part II

The Philosophy of Freedom

In this section I present those papers in which I have attempted to set forth exactly what I stand for and why. The first paper, "The Case for Economic Freedom," was given as a speech on numerous occasions (particularly at seminars organized by the Foundation for Economic Education at Irvington, New York) before being put down on paper. The second paper was originally prepared for an appearance before the students and faculty of the college where I teach, Wabash College, and was my attempt to tell them the kind of person (in Rogge) they were harboring in their midst. "Who's to Blame" was presented to an even earlier convocation at Wabash College, at a time when I was serving as Dean of the College. It is presented as a further development of the idea of personal responsibility discussed in the first two papers of this section.

"Paradise in Posey County" was another of my chapel messages to young men; in it I explore (and criticize) the idea of Utopia as displayed in two famous experiments in communal living in Indiana.

Chapter 1

The Case for Economic Freedom

My economic philosophy is here offered with full knowledge that it is *not* generally accepted as the right one. On the contrary, my brand of economics has now become *Brand X,* the one that is never selected as the whitest by the housewife, the one that is said to be slow acting, the one that contains no miracle ingredient. It loses nine times out of ten in the popularity polls run on Election Day, and, in most elections, it doesn't even present a candidate.

I shall identify my brand of economics as that of economic freedom, and I shall define economic freedom as that set of economic arrangements that would exist in a society in which the government's only function would be to prevent one man from using force or fraud against another—including within this, of course, the task of national defense. So that there can be no misunderstanding here, let me say that this is pure, uncompromising *laissez faire* economics. It is not the mixed economy; it is the unmixed economy.

I readily admit that I do not expect to see such an economy in my lifetime or in anyone's lifetime in the infinity of years ahead of us. I present it rather as the ideal we should strive for and should be disappointed in never fully attaining.

Where do we find the most powerful and persuasive case for economic freedom? I don't know; probably it hasn't been prepared as yet. Certainly it is unlikely that the case I present is the definitive one. However, it is the one that is persuasive with me, that leads me to my own deep commitment to the free market. I present it as grist for your own mill and not as the divinely inspired last word on the subject.

The Moral Case

You will note as I develop my case that I attach relatively little importance to the demonstrated efficiency of the free-market system in promoting economic growth, in raising levels of living. In fact, my central thesis is that *the most important part of the case for economic freedom is not its vaunted efficiency as a system for organizing resources, not its dramatic success in promoting economic growth, but rather its consistency with certain fundamental moral principles of life itself.*

I say, "the most important part of the case" for two reasons. First, the significance I attach to those moral principles would lead me to prefer the free enterprise system even if it were demonstrably less efficient than alternative systems, even if it were to produce a *slower* rate of economic growth than systems of central direction and control. Second, the great mass of the people of any country is never really going to understand the purely economic workings of *any* economic system, be it free enterprise or socialism. Hence, most people are going to judge an economic system by its consistency with their moral principles rather than by its purely scientific operating characteristics. If economic freedom survives in the years ahead, it will be only because a majority of the people accept its basic morality. The success of the system in bringing ever higher levels of living will be no more persuasive in the future than it has been in the past. Let me illustrate.

The doctrine of man held in general in nineteenth-century America argued that each man was ultimately responsible for what happened to him, for his own salvation, both in the here and now and in the hereafter. Thus, whether a man prospered or failed in economic life was each man's individual responsibility: each man had a right to the rewards for success and, in the same sense, deserved the punishment that came with failure. It followed as well that it is explicitly immoral to use the power of government to take from one man to give to another, to legalize Robin Hood. This doctrine of man found its economic counterpart in the system of free enterprise and, hence, the system of free enterprise was accepted and respected by many who had no real understanding of its subtleties as a technique for organizing resource use.

As this doctrine of man was replaced by one which made of man a helpless victim of his subconscious and his environment—responsible for neither his successes nor his failures—the free enterprise system came to be rejected by many who still had no real understanding of its actual operating characteristics.

Basic Values Considered

Inasmuch as my own value systems and my own assumptions about human beings are so important to the case, I want to sketch them for you.

To begin with, the central value in my choice system is individual freedom. By freedom I mean exactly and only freedom from coercion by others. I do not mean the four freedoms of President Roosevelt, which are not freedoms at all, but only rhetorical devices to persuade people to give up some of their true freedom. In the Rogge system, each man must be free to do what is his duty as he defines it, so long as he does not use force against another.

Next, I believe each man to be ultimately responsible for what happens to him. True, he is influenced by his heredity, his environment, his subconscious, and by pure chance. But I insist that precisely what makes man man is his ability to rise above these influences, to change and determine his own destiny. If this be true, then it follows that each of us is terribly and inevitably and forever responsible for everything he does. The answer to the question, "Who's to blame?" is always, "*Mea culpa,* I am."

I believe as well that man is imperfect, now and forever. He is imperfect in his knowledge of the ultimate purpose of his life, imperfect in his choice of means to serve those purposes he does select, imperfect in the integrity with which he deals with himself and those around him, imperfect in his capacity to love his fellow man. If man is imperfect, then all of his constructs must be imperfect, and the choice is always among degrees and kinds of imperfection. The New Jerusalem is never going to be realized here on earth, and the man who insists that it is, is always lost unto freedom.

Moreover, man's imperfections are intensified as he acquires the power to coerce others; "power tends to corrupt and absolute power corrupts absolutely."

This completes the listing of my assumptions, and it should be clear that the list does not constitute a total philosophy of life. Most importantly, it does not define what I believe the free man's *duty* to be, or more specifically, what I believe my own duty to be and the source of the charge to me. However important these questions, I do not consider them relevant to the choice of an economic system.

Here, then, are two sections of the case for economic freedom as I would construct it. The first section presents economic freedom as an ultimate end in itself and the second presents it as a means to the preservation of the noneconomic elements in total freedom.

Individual Freedom of Choice

The first section of the case is made in the stating of it, if one accepts the fundamental premise.

Major premise: Each man should be free to take whatever *action* he wishes, so long as he does not use force or fraud against another.

Minor premise: All economic behavior is "action" as identified above.

Conclusion: Each man should be free to take whatever action he wishes in his economic behavior, so long as he does not use force or fraud against another.

In other words, economic freedom is a part of total freedom; *if freedom is an end in itself, as our society has traditionally asserted it to be, then economic freedom is an end in itself, to be valued for itself alone and not just for its instrumental value in serving other goals.*

If this thesis is accepted, then there must aways exist a tremendous presumption against each and every proposal for governmental limitation of economic freedom. What is wrong with a state system of compulsory social security? It denies to the individual his *freedom,* his right to choose what he will do with his own money resources. What is wrong with a governmentally enforced minimum wage? It denies to the employer and the employee their individual freedoms, their individual rights to enter into voluntary relationships not involving force or fraud. What is wrong with a tariff or an import quota? It denies to the individual consumer his right to buy what he wishes, wherever he wishes.

It is breathtaking to think what this simple approach would do to the apparatus of state control at all levels of government. Strike from the books all legislation that denies economic freedom to any individual, and three-fourths of all the activities now undertaken by government would be eliminated.

I am no dreamer of empty dreams, and I do not expect that the day will ever come when this principle of economic freedom as a part of total freedom will be fully accepted and applied. Yet I am convinced that unless this principle is given some standing, unless those who examine proposals for new regulation of the individual by government look on this loss of freedom as a "cost" of the proposed legislation, the chances of free enterprise surviving are small indeed. The would-be controller can always find reasons why it might seem expedient to control the individual; unless slowed down by some general feeling that it is immoral to do so, he will usually have his way.

Noneconomic Freedoms

So much for the first section of the case. Now for the second. The major premise here is the same, that is, the premise of the rightness of freedom. Here, though, the concern is with the noneconomic elements in total freedom—with freedom of speech, of religion, of the press, of personal behavior. My thesis is that these freedoms are not likely to be long preserved in a society that has denied economic freedom to its individual members.

Before developing this thesis, I wish to comment briefly on the importance of these noneconomic freedoms. I do so because we who are known as conservatives have often given too little attention to these freedoms or have even played a significant role in reducing them. The modern liberal is usually inconsistent in that he defends man's noneconomic freedoms, but is often quite indifferent to his economic freedom. The modern conservative is often inconsistent in that he defends man's economic freedom but is indifferent to his noneconomic freedoms. Why are there so few conservatives in the struggles over censorship, over denials of equality before the law for people of all races, over blue laws, and so on? Why do we let the modern liberals dominate an organization such as the American Civil Liberties Union? The general purposes of this organization are completely consistent with, even necessary to, the truly free society.

Particularly in times of stress such as these, we must fight against the general pressure to curb the rights of individual human beings, even those whose ideas and actions we detest. Now is the time to remember the example of men such as David Ricardo, the London banker and economist of the classical free-market school in the first part of the last century. Born a Jew, married to a Quaker, he devoted some part of his energy and his fortune to eliminating the legal discrimination against Catholics in the England of his day.

It is precisely because I believe these noneconomic freedoms to be so important that I believe economic freedom to be so important. The argument here could be drawn from the wisdom of the Bible and the statement that "where a man's treasure is, there will his heart be also." Give me control over a man's economic actions, and hence over his means of survival, and except for a few occasional heroes, I'll promise to deliver to you men who think and write and behave as I want them to.

The case is not difficult to make for the fully controlled economy, the true socialistic state. Milton Friedman, professor of economics at the University of Chicago, in his book, *Capitalism and Freedom,* takes the case of a socialist society that has a sincere desire to preserve the freedom of the press. The first problem would be that there would be no private capital, no private fortunes that could be used to subsidize an antisocialist, procapitalist press. Hence, the socialist state would have to do it. However, the men and women undertaking the task would have to be released from the socialist labor pool and would have to be assured that they would never be discriminated against in employment opportunities in the socialist apparatus if they were to wish to change occupations later. Then these procapitalist members of the socialist society would have to go to other functionaries of the state to secure the buildings, the presses, the paper, the skilled and unskilled workmen, and all the other components of a working newspaper. Then they would face the problem of finding distribution outlets, either creating their own (a frightening task) or using the same ones used by the official socialist propaganda organs. Finally, where would they find readers? How many men and women would risk showing up at their state-controlled jobs carrying copies of the *Daily Capitalist?*

There are so many unlikely steps in this process that the assumption that true freedom of the press could be maintained in a socialist society is so unrealistic as to be ludicrous.

Partly Socialized

Of course, we are not facing as yet a fully socialized America, but only one in which there is significant government intervention in a still predominantly private enterprise economy. Do these interventions pose any threat to the noneconomic freedoms? I believe they do.

First of all, the total of coercive devices now available to any administration of either party at the national level is so great that true freedom to work actively against the current administration (whatever it might be) is seriously reduced. For example, farmers have become captives of the government in such a way that they are forced into political alignments that seriously reduce their ability to protest actions they do not approve. The new trade bill, though right in the principle of free trade, gives to the President enormous power to reward his friends and punish his critics.

Second, the form of these interventions is such as to threaten seriously one of the real cornerstones of all freedoms—equality before the law. For example, farmers and trade union members are now encouraged and assisted in doing precisely that for which businessmen are sent to jail (i.e., acting collusively to manipulate prices). The blindfolded Goddess of Justice has been encouraged to peek and she now says, with the jurists of the ancient regime, "First tell me who you are and then I'll tell you what your rights are." A society in which such gross inequalities before the law are encouraged in economic life is not likely to be one which preserves the principle of equality before the law generally.

We could go on to many specific illustrations. For example, the government uses its legislated monopoly to carry the mails as a means for imposing a censorship on what people send to each other in a completely voluntary relationship. A man and a woman who exchange obscene letters may not be making productive use of their time, but their correspondence is certainly no business of the government. Or to take an example from another country, Winston Churchill, as a critic of the Chamberlain government, was not permitted one minute of radio time on the government-owned and monopolized broadcasting system in the period from 1936 to the outbreak of the war he was predicting in 1939.

Each Step Leads to Another

Every act of intervention in the economic life of its citizens gives to a government additional power to shape and control the attitudes, the writings, the behavior of those citizens. Every such act is another break in the dike protecting the integrity of the individual as a free man or woman.

The free market protects the integrity of the individual by providing him with a host of decentralized alternatives rather than with one centralized opportunity. As Friedman has reminded us, even the known communist can readily find employment in capitalist America. The free market is politics-blind, religion-blind, and, yes, race-blind. Do you ask about the politics or the religion of the farmer who grew the potatoes you buy at the store? Do you ask about the color of the hands that helped produce the steel you use in your office building?

South Africa provides an interesting example of this.

The South Africans, of course, provide a shocking picture of racial bigotry, shocking even to a country that has its own tragic race problems. South African law clearly separates the whites from the nonwhites. Orientals have traditionally been classed as nonwhites, but South African trade with Japan has become so important in the postwar period that the government of South Africa has declared the Japanese visitors to South Africa to be officially and legally "white." The free market is one of the really great forces making for tolerance and understanding among human beings. The controlled market gives man rein to express all those blind prejudices and intolerant beliefs to which he is forever subject.

Impersonality of the Market

To look at this another way: The free market is often said to be impersonal, and indeed it is. Rather than a vice, this is one of its great virtues. Because the relations *are* substantially impersonal, they are not usually marked by bitter personal conflict. It is precisely because the labor union attempts to take the employment relationship *out* of the marketplace that bitter personal conflict so often marks union-management relationships. The intensely personal relationship is one that is civilized only by love, as between man and wife, and within the family. But man's capacity for love is severely limited by his imperfect nature. Far better, then, to economize on love, to reserve our dependence on it to those relationships where even our imperfect natures are capable of sustained action based on love. Far better, then, to build our economic system on largely impersonal relationships and on man's self-interest—a motive power with which he is generously supplied. One need only study the history of such utopian experiments as our Indiana's Harmony and New Harmony to realize that a social structure which ignores man's essential nature results in the dissension, conflict, disintegration, and dissolution of Robert Owen's New Harmony or the absolutism of Father Rapp's Harmony.

The "vulgar calculus of the marketplace," as its critics have described it, is still the most humane way man has yet found for solving those questions of economic allocation and division which are ubiquitous in human society. By what must seem fortunate coincidence, it is also the system most likely to produce the affluent society, to move mankind above an existence in which life is mean, nasty, brutish, and short. But, of course, this is *not* just coincidence. Under economic freedom, only man's destructive instincts are curbed by law. All of his creative instincts are released and freed to work those wonders of which free men are capable. In the controlled society only the creativity of the few at the top can be utilized, and much of this creativity must be expended in maintaining control and in fending off rivals. In the free society, the creativity of every man can be expressed—and surely by now we know that we cannot predict who will prove to be the most creative.

You may be puzzled, then, that I do not rest my case for economic freedom on its productive achievements; on its buildings, its houses, its automobiles, its bathtubs, its wonder drugs, its television sets, its sirloin steaks and green salads with Roquefort dressings. I neither feel within myself nor do I hear in the testimony of others any evidence that man's search for purpose, his longing for fulfillment, is in any significant way relieved by these accomplishments. I do not scorn these accomplishments nor do I worship them. Nor do I find in the lives of those who do worship them any evidence that thcy find ultimate peace and justification in their idols.

I rest my case rather on the consistency of the free market with man's essential nature, on the basic morality of its system of rewards and punishments, on the protection it gives to the integrity of the individual.

The free market cannot produce the perfect world, but it can create an environment in which each imperfect man may conduct his lifelong search for purpose in his own way, in which each day he may order his life according to his own imperfect vision of his destiny, suffering both the agonies of his errors and the sweet pleasure of his successes. This freedom is what it means to be a man; this is the God-head, if you wish.

I give you, then, the free market, the expression of man's economic freedom and the guarantor of all his other freedoms.

Chapter 2

The Libertarian Philosophy

I intend to spend the next seventeen minutes answering a question that a disappointingly small number of people even bother to ask. The question is this: Just what *is* Ben Rogge's social philosophy? or to put it the way a few who have heard me speak have put it: "Rogge, just what kind of a nut are you?" This way of putting it, although accurate perhaps, is distressing to me because I am essentially a button-down-collar, Kiwanis Club-type conformist. My only attention-drawing eccentricity has been a tendency to give myself all putts under five feet.

But I suppose that any man must expect to create both suspicion and confusion when he demands, at one and the same time, that prostitution be legalized, that the social security system be abolished, that the laws making it a crime to use marijuana be repealed, along with the laws against child labor, and that we sell Yellowstone Park to the people who operate Disneyland.

This is indeed a mixed bag, but it is my very own bag and to me these apparently diverse elements represent simply different applications of a single guiding principle. To anticipate, this principle is that each man and each woman should be permitted to do his or her thing, singly or in pairs or in groups as large as the Mormon Church or General Motors, so long as it's peaceful.

Now, to the heart of the matter. First, is my social philosophy properly described as one of the competing ideologies of our day? To this the answer is no. In the first place, it is so far out of fashion that it can hardly be said to be competing; second, it is thought by many to be not of our day, but of the last century; and third, I see it as not an ideology at all but rather the negation of ideology. I quote now from Webster's New Collegiate Dictionary: "*ideology*—the integrated assertions, theories and aims constituting a politico-social program." To me, this identifies the ideologue as someone, be he Christian or Moslem or Marxist or Fascist or Liberal Reformer or Monarchist, who has a clear vision of what man is or should be or could become and who has some kind of socio-political program for bringing about the desired state of affairs. To the ideologue, the ideal social system is to be defined in terms of certain ends or goals to be attained, such as the elimination of poverty or the elimination of racial prejudice or the maximizing of the growth rate or the establishment of one true religion or the dominance of the master race or the implementation of the General Will or the eternal glory of the American or the French nation. Usually, but not always, there are certain restraints placed on the means to be used, but the emphasis is upon the vision of the proper goal of man's existence here on earth, as revealed by voices from burning bushes or by prophets or by the magnificently objective results of science or in the massive and blind forces of history or in the dark and mysterious processes of the human mind or what-have-you.

To the libertarian, in a certain sense, *it is not the ends of man's actions that count but only the means used in serving those ends.* To each of the ideologues he says: "You may be right and you may keep on trying to convince me and others that you are right, *but* the only means you may use are those of persuasion. You may not impose your vision *by force* on anyone. This means not only that you are not to stone the prostitute or the hippie or the college dean or the Jew or the businessman or even the policeman; it means as well, and most importantly, that you are not to get the policeman or the sheriff to do your stoning for you."

In saying this, the libertarian is not necessarily declaring himself to be agnostic in his attitude toward any and all ideologies. He may in fact have some clear preferences as among ideologies. At the same time, men who feel deeply about something are rarely tolerant with respect to that something. I, Ben Rogge, do not use marijuana nor do I approve of its use, but I am afraid that if I support laws against its use, some fool will insist as well on denying me my noble and useful gin and tonic. I believe that the typical Episcopal Church is somewhat higher on the scale of civilization than the snake-handling cults of West Virginia. Frankly I wouldn't touch even a consecrated reptile with a ten-foot pole, or even a nine-iron, but as far as the Anglican Church is concerned, I am still an anti-anti-disestablishmentarian, if you know what I mean.

Well, so what? How does all this set the libertarian apart (whether for better or for worse) from all others? Let us take first the traditionalist or conservative, with whom the libertarian is often linked, largely erroneously. True, together they sing the chorus of damn the unions, damn the minimum wage laws, and damn the progressive income tax. But when the libertarian starts a chorus of damn the Sunday blue laws, he ends up singing a solo.

Let me be careful about this. What I am asking for is precisely when men like Albert Jay Nock have asked for in the past—that *the society* be distinguished from *the state* and that the society not be absorbed by the state. Society, with its full network of restraints on individual conduct, based on custom, tradition, religion, personal morality, a sense of style, and with all of its indeed powerful sanctions, is what makes the civilized life possible and meaningful. I am not proposing an anarchic society; on the contrary *I am essentially a conservative on most questions of social organization and social process*. I do believe in continuity, in the important role of tradition and custom, in standards for personal conduct, in the great importance of the elites (imperfect though they may be).

But unlike the political conservative, I do not wish to see these influences on individual behavior institutionalized in the hands of the state. As I read history, I see that everywhere the generally accepted social processes have been made into law, civilization has ceased to advance. For one, the penalty to be paid by the innovator, which is severe even *without* the law, and perhaps properly so, is made so severe (even including death) as to stop that healthy and necessary and slow process of change through which civilizations move to higher levels of achievement.

For another, the elites, if given the power to implement their views with the use of force, are almost certain to be corrupted by that power and to cease playing their essential and beneficial role in society. The pages of history are strewn with the wreckages of superior men who have been undone by the corrupting influence of possession of the power to coerce.

Now to the modern liberal. How does the libertarian differ from the modern liberal? Well, he cuts in where the conservative cuts out and cuts out where the conservative cuts in. Like the libertarian, the modern liberal is all for sin, so long as it's peaceful. But unlike the libertarian, the modern liberal is perfectly willing to use the sheriff to attempt to bring about whatever outcomes he desires in economic life. Should there be a Pure Books, Plays and Films administration? Never, says the modern liberal. Should there be a Pure Food and Drug Administration? Of course, says the modern liberal. If two consenting adults engage in an unnatural act in private, should the law intervene? Never, says the modern liberal. If two consenting adults arrive at a wage contract calling for the payment of $1.00 an hour to the one, should the state intervene and require that the payment must be no less than $1.60 per hour (even if, by the very act, that leads to no contract; to no job at all)? Of course, says the modern liberal. These examples could be multiplied indefinitely.

Now perhaps there are real differences in circumstances that make these differences in evaluation consistent. Perhaps the modern liberal is right and the libertarian is wrong. What I am trying to point out is that the libertarian is opposed to intervention by the state in *any* of the peaceful actions of individuals or groups, whether the relationship involves sex, games, or the marketplace, and this sets him apart from both the modern conservative and the modern liberal.

Now what of the New Left? Here too there are some family resemblances, and some of my libertarian friends are now involved in a love affair with the New Left, such as writing for *Ramparts* magazine and lecturing at the Free University in New York. In some ways this makes sense. The New Left and the libertarians share a common suspicion of concentrated power, and particularly of the power to coerce; they join in not wishing to be ruled by any establishment, even of the elite. But there the love affair comes to an abrupt end.

To the libertarian, private property is an extension of the human personality and an absolutely necessary element in the structure of a society of free men; to the New Lefter, private property is largely an invention of the establishment to suppress the free human spirit and is a barrier to the full expression of human concern and relatedness. To the libertarian, or at least to Ben Rogge, the "politics of confrontation" is neither peaceful as a means nor acceptable as an end, if the end is what it so often seems to be, the imposing of a minority view on the majority by what amounts to blackmail. "Give in to my demands and I'll leave your office; throw me off your property and you are guilty of breaking the peace. Call in the cops to protect that which is yours and you are a fascist." To the libertarian this is nonsense and very dangerous nonsense indeed. The goal of the victory of persuasion over force in human affairs can hardly be well served by what amounts to the use of force.

But of course the goal of the New Left is not the goal of the libertarian—the right choice of means. In fact the goals of the New Left are difficult to identify, particularly in terms of the kind of social arrangements they wish to see brought into being out of the ashes of that which we now have. There seem to be three main possibilities: (1) an essentially anarchist arrangement, with no government; (2) a syndicalist-communalist arrangement, with minimal government; or (3) an out-and-out Marxist-socialist dictatorship of the proletariat. To the libertarian, the first would soon become the tyranny of the strong, and life would indeed be mean, nasty, brutish and short; the second would mean economic chaos and starvation for most; the third would mean tyranny, bold and bloody and bright.

To all of these—the conservative, the modern liberal, and the New Left—the libertarian says, with Huckleberry Finn, "No thank you, I have been there before." He insists that what marks the civilized society is not so much *what* goals its people are seeking as what *means* are used and accepted in the seeking of goals. He insists that to the opinions and ideas and revelations of even the best of men must still cling the mortal, the human uncertainty. If even those who come to be least imperfect in knowing and acting cannot be identified in advance (or even clearly identified after the fact), surely it follows that each imperfect man must be given (indeed, *has*) the right to follow his own imperfectly selected star in his own imperfect way, to march to the music that *he* hears and not to the music that you and I hear.

The libertarian is in no sense a utopian. He argues only that in a world in which each individual, imperfect man was left free to make his own imperfect decisions and to act on them in any way that is peaceful, enjoying the fruits of his successes and suffering the agony of his mistakes, man could at least fully attain to the dignity and tragedy and comedy that comes with being a man. And here, somewhere east of Eden, there is little more that we can expect out of life.

Chapter 3

Who's to Blame?

In some 63.7 percent of all interviews in my office, the person across the desk is there to tell me who's to blame. And in 99.6 percent of the cases where that is the question, the answer is the same: *He* isn't.

Now if these were just simple cases of prevarication, we could all shake our heads at the loss of the old Yes-father-I-chopped-down-the-cherry-tree spirit and turn to some other problem, such as the danger presented to the stability of the earth by the buildup of snow on the polar icecaps. But the denial of responsibility is rarely that simple, and herein lies the story.

Today's George Washington, on the campus and elsewhere, says, "Yes, I chopped down the cherry tree, *but*—" and then comes ten to ninety minutes of explanation, which is apparently supposed to end in my breaking into tears and forgiving all, after which he goes home to sharpen his little hatchet.

The little Georges of today say, "Yes, I chopped

down the cherry tree, but let me give you the *whole* story. All the guys over at the house were telling me that it's a tradition around here to cut down cherry trees. What's that? Did any of *them* ever actually cut down any cherry trees? Well, I don't know, but anyway there's this tradition, see, and with all this lack of school spirit, I figured I was really doing the school a favor when I cut down that crummy old tree." [*Lights up, center stage, where our hero is receiving a medal from the president of the Student Council as the band plays the school song.*]

Or it may run like this: "Now this professor, see, told us to collect some forest specimens; he may have told us what trees to cut, but, frankly, I just can't understand half of what he says, and I honestly thought he said cherry tree. Now actually I wasn't in class the day he gave the assignment and this friend of mine took it down and I can't help it if he made a mistake can I? Anyway, if the callboy had awakened me on time, I'd have made the class and would have known he said to get leaves from a whortleberry bush."

Society on Trial

So far we have run through the simpler cases. Now let's move to more complex ones. In this one, little George says to his father, "Yes, Dad, I cut down the cherry tree, but I just couldn't help it. You and mother are always away from home and when you are home all you do is tell me to get out of the house, to go practice throwing a dollar across the Rappahannock. I guess I cut down the tree to get you to pay a little attention to me, and you can't blame me for that, can you?" [*Lights up, center stage, revealing the kindly old judge admonishing the parents to show more love and affection to little George, who is seated right, quietly hacking away at the jury box.*]

These can get messy. Here's another. In this one, young George has hired himself a slick city lawyer who has read all the recent books on the sociology of crime. The lawyer pleads G.W.'s case as follows: "It is true that this young man cut down the tree, marked exhibit A and lying there on the first ten rows of the courtroom seats. Also, there can be no question but that he did it willfully and maliciously, nor can it be denied that he has leveled over half the cherry trees in northern Virginia in exactly the same way. But is this boy to blame? Can he be held responsible for his actions? No. The real crime is his society's, and not his. He is the product of his environment, the victim of a social system which breeds crime in every form. Born in poverty, raised in the slums, abused by his parents," and on and on. The lawyer closes by pointing a finger at me and saying dramatically, "You, Dean Rogge, as a member of the society which has produced this young monster, are as much to blame as he, as much deserving of punishment as he." The boy gets off with a six-month suspended sentence and I am ridden out of town on a rail.

I do want to refer to just one other possibility. In this one, the lawyer calls as a witness an eminent psychoanalyst who, as a result of his examination of the young man, absolves him of all conscious responsibility for the crime, in testimony that is filled with the jargon of that semi-science—hence obscure, hence somewhat pornographic. It turns out that the cherry tree is a phallic symbol and the boy's action an unconscious and perverse response to the universal castration complex.

Farfetched? Not at all. As Richard LaPiere writes in his book, *The Freudian Ethic:*

> The Freudian explanation of crime absolves the individual from all personal responsibility for the criminal act and places the blame squarely upon the shoulders of an abstraction—society. Modern society is especially hard upon the individual, since it imposes upon him so many and often contradictory restraints and at the same time demands of him so much that does not come naturally to him. His criminal acts are therefore but a symptom of the underlying pathology of society, and it is as futile to punish him for the sins of society as to attempt to cure acne by medicating the symptomatic pustules.

Responsibility Is Personal

Where does all this leave us? Who's to blame? Well, nobody, or rather everybody. The Freudian ethic has eliminated sin (and, of course, that means that it has eliminated virtue as well).

Personally, I can't buy it. I cannot accept a view of man which makes him a helpless pawn of either his id or his society. I do not deny that the mind of each of us is a dark and complex chamber, nor that the individual is bent by his environment, nor even the potentially baneful influence of parents. As a matter of fact, after a few months in the dean's office, I was ready to recommend to the college that henceforth it admit only orphans. But as a stubborn act of faith I insist that precisely what makes man man is his potential ability to conquer both himself and his environment. If this capacity is indeed given to or possessed by each of us, then it follows that we are inevitably and terribly and forever responsible for everything that we do. The answer to the question, "Who's to blame?" is always, "Mea Culpa, I am."

This is a tough philosophy. The Christian can take hope in the thought that though his sins can never be excused, he may still come under the grace of God, sinner though he be. The non-Christian has to find some other source of strength, and believe me, this is not easy to do.

What does all this have to do with our day-to-day living, whether on or beyond the campus? Actually, it has everything to do with it. It means that as students we stop blaming our teachers, our classmates, our parents, our high schools, our society, and even the callboy for our own mistakes and shortcomings. It means that as teachers and college administrators we stop blaming our students, the board of trustees, the oppressive spirit of society (and even our wives) for our own failures.

As individuals it means that we stop making excuses to ourselves, that we carry each cherry tree we cut down on our consciences forever. It means that we say with Cassius, "The fault, dear Brutus, is not in the stars, but in ourselves." This is a tough philosophy, but it is also the only hopeful one man has yet devised.

Chapter 4

Paradise in Posey County

In these comments I offer three morality tales for your guidance, with the moral to be found in each tailored to the needs of my pre-existing biases. My first and third stories are laid in that romantic region, Posey County in Indiana's pocket country—once the haunt of Ohio River pirates and moonshiners. My second is laid in the no-less-romantic home of Bobbie Burns, oatmeal, and the theory of infant damnation—to be specific, in New Lanark, Scotland.

One early summer day in 1815, a strange and wonderful armada entered the mouth of the Wabash River. In the lead boat, somewhat obscured by a magnificent patriarchal beard, stood Father Rapp, the leader of this valiant group. In the other boats were some eight hundred men, women, and older children. All were dressed in the quaint costume of German peasants from the region of Wurttemberg. This is not surprising because that is just what they were.

They went ashore just a few miles up the Wabash from its mouth and, kneeling in prayer, dedicated "Harmony" (the name they had selected for their settlement) to the uses of Christian brotherhood. These were the Rappites—German peasants, primitive Christians, practical communists, and the followers of George Rapp. Why were there only older children in the group, you ask? Because some years before they had sworn themselves to celibacy. The reason? God had originally made Adam as part male, part female. The separation of the one into two had led to the fall from grace; hence the celibate state is more pleasing to God. (No man or woman who has been married for any considerable time would wish to reject that hypothesis out of hand.)

These people were also millennialists. They believed that the coming of the One was imminent and that when He came He would deal out destruction to all of man's futile and evil creations. Particularly marked for destruction was Pittsburgh, Pennsylvania, near which the Rappites had lived for their first ten years in America and from the citizens of which city they had apparently suffered numerous indignities. Unfortunately, perhaps, Pittsburgh still stands, sustained no doubt by the combined strength of the United States Steel Company and Mean Joe Greene.

Arising from their knees, where we have kept them for too long, these sturdy souls set to work with a will to bring order to the wilderness. How well they succeeded can be seen in the fact that ten years later

Harmony was clearly the most prosperous place in the entire region. The Rappites sold their many products throughout the Mississippi valley—wheat, hides, horses, hogs, shingles, linen, tobacco, furniture, and whiskey reputed to be the best in the West—a whiskey that they themselves were forbidden even to sample for taste. They had their stores in Vincennes, Shawneetown, and St. Louis, with agents in Pittsburgh, Louisville, and New Orleans.

How were these miracles accomplished at a time when Indianapolis was a wilderness and Fort Wayne a place where the whites dressed like Indians and wore scalps at their belts? By a shrewd mixture of communism, the capitalist marketplace, religion, superstition, and the autocratic driving force of George Rapp. Rapp taught his followers obedience, humility, and self-sacrifice; he also used every trick in the bag—not excluding force—to keep his followers in line. We are told (in a probably apocryphal story) that when his only blood-line son broke the vow of celibacy, he had him forcibly emasculated, and the impetuous young man died in the process. Rapp also had frequent visitations from obliging angels who told him what his followers must do. The footprints of one of the heavier of those angels can still be seen impressed in a limestone slab in modern New Harmony (the angel involved was no less than the angel Gabriel). He also had built various tunnels under the settlement, and the young Rappite who thought that he might rest for a moment, perhaps to reflect on the dubious privilege of celibacy, might find himself confronted with the furry head of his ubiquitous leader, emerging from the bowels of the earth to reproach him for having yielded to temptation.

In 1825, Rapp, discouraged by the unfriendly nature of the malaria-bearing mosquitoes and the citizens of Evansville and Princeton who surrounded him, decided to move his flock again and sold the whole operation for $150,000. He led his followers back toward the hated Pittsburgh, where they founded a new community, appropriately labeled Economy.

So much for the first story. Now for the second. It starts on January 1, 1780, in New Lanark, Scotland. A rising young industrialist, Robert Owen, has just assumed control of the New Lanark textile mills. In a new twist on an old story, now that Owen and his partners have purchased the mills, he marries the daughter of the previous owner.

Robert Owen also sees visions, but instead of visions of the millennium, he envisions a paradise here on earth, "a new existence to man" to be attained by surrounding him with superior circumstances only. The mind of the child is a blank page, a *tabula rasa,* says Owen; let only the rational, the pleasant, the good be written on that page, and the world can be transformed in one generation.

Unrealistic? Impractical? Not so, says Owen, and goes to work on the people of New Lanark, particularly the children. He reduces the hours of work in the mills, organizes schools for the children (where the two teachers can neither read nor write and hence are uncorrupted by unnatural, non-Rousseau mankind), replaces the whip in the mills with various colored blocks which indicate whether a given worker has been good or bad, and sends his inspectors to check on the cleanliness of each home. This his fellow industrialists might have forgiven him had he not also made an incredible amount of money in the process. His textiles command a 50 percent premium in the market and he recoups his investment in four years' time. Philanthropy is proved to be practical, and modern industrial psychology is born. From Russia comes Grand Duke Nicholas to survey the wonders of New Lanark. The Duke of Kent, whose daughter is to rule England for over sixty years, and who is neither more nor less off his rocker than the other offspring of that addled rustic, George III, is an enthusiastic disciple of Owen's and a close personal friend. New Lanark is soon known throughout the world.

For most men this would be enough, but Owen is a born chaser after the immortal butterfly. New Lanark today; the world tomorrow. In his book, *New View of Society,* he presents his science of society, complete with a rational deistic religion, modified free love, abolition of private property, and rectangular communities of two thousand people. Goaded by his critics, he determines to prove the practicability of his scheme, and in 1824 he completes arrangements to buy our old friend, Harmony, from the Rappites for $150,000. Thus, New Harmony is launched, and with it our third story.

This third story is short, like the life-span of the experiment it describes. No model community was ever launched with more fanfare. In the early spring of 1825, Robert Owen delivered an address in Washington, D.C., on his plans to redeem the world. In the audience were most members of both houses of Congress, the judges of the Supreme Court, President John Quincy Adams, and most of his cabinet members. An invitation was issued to all who shared Owen's desire for a new state of society to join him in New Harmony. Many responded, including some of the best-educated men of the day.

The old Harmony had been composed of ignorant, superstitious peasants. New Harmony was composed of many men of brilliance, including of course Robert Owen, the leading industrialist of the world. The Rappites had had to tame a wilderness. The Owenites were moved into one of the most prosperous pieces of real estate west of the mountains. The Rappites were just putting in their time until the world came to an end; the Owenites were launching the Brave New World. The Rappite settlement lasted ten years and was many times more prosperous when it ended than when it began. The New Harmony experiment lasted less than three years and was a social and financial disaster.

It is instructive to follow the chronology of events.

After his triumph in Washington, Owen made his way to New Harmony. In April 1825, in the old Rappite church, he announced, "I am come to this country to introduce an entire new system of society; to change it from an ignorant, selfish system to an enlightened social system which shall gradually unite all interests into one, and remove all causes for contest between individuals." He proposed to establish a "new empire of peace and goodwill," which would lead to "that state of virtue, intelligence, enjoyment and happiness which it has been foretold by the sages of the past would at some time become the lot of man." The truth of his principles would spread "from Community to Community, from State to State, from Continent to Continent, finally overshadowing the whole earth, shedding light, fragrance and abundance, intelligence and happiness upon the sons of man." Here is the way it was expressed in an Owenite poem:

Ah, soon will come the glorious day,
   Inscribed on Mercy's brow,
When truth shall rend the veil away
   That blinds the nations now.

The face of man shall wisdom learn,
   And error cease to reign:
The charms of innocence return,
   And all be new again.[1]

[1] Mark Holloway, *Heavens on Earth: Utopian Communities in America 1680–1880,* 2d ed. (New York: Peter Smith, 1966), p. 101.

However, Owen was no foolish optimist; he did not expect this to come about immediately; on the contrary, he admitted that the whole task would probably take at least three years. He then offered the community a constitution (which provided for something less than the ultimate communism), appointed a Preliminary Committee to manage the affairs of the society, issued an invitation to "the industrious and well-disposed of all nations" to come to New Harmony—and promptly took off for England.

Many did respond to this generous invitation, but I must report to you, in sadness, that not all who did so were "industrious" or "well-disposed." Some were indeed attracted by the intellectual excitement of the society—but were less than excited by the associated labor in the dairy barns. Others were drawn by the alluring combination of free food and free love—neither of which proved in fact to be readily or long available in New Harmony.

In the meantime, though, sustained by the generosity of Robert Owen and William Maclure (a scholarly and wealthy convert to Owenism), the society managed to survive through 1825. The *New Harmony Gazette* (the uncritical voice of Owen's philosophy and Owen's optimism) reported that various businesses and manufacturers were "doing well" but regrettably only "soap and glue" were produced in quantities that "exceeded consumption." Both medicines and basic foods were available without cost . . . except, of course, to Owen.

One hundred and thirty children were schooled, boarded, and clothed at public (i.e., Owen's) expense. Amusements flourished. A band played for a ball each Tuesday night and for a concert each Friday night, both in the old Rappite church—which, I regret to report, was no longer used for the purposes for which it had been so lovingly constructed by the Rappites.

Owen returned to New Harmony in January of 1826, and growing impatient with the step-by-step approach to paradise, proclaimed "The New Harmony Community of Equality," under the direction of an Executive Council, soon to be replaced, at the request of the membership, by one-man rule by Owen himself. A nucleus of twenty-five of the true believers was created and all others had to apply anew for membership in the community (with Owen having the right of veto). It is instructive to note that there were three classes of memberships outside the nucleus—conditional, probationary, and persons on trial. If a Paradise on Earth, why not a Purgatory as well?

By May of 1826, two communities of dissenters had been established: Macluria and Feiba Pavelli. Those great friends, Owen and Maclure, had come to a parting of the ways over the proper conduct of the educational program. Maclure, a disciple of Pestolozzi, had not followed Owen's instructions in the education of the young, and the result was a new colony, across the road from the old. Feiba Pavelli was formed largely by a group of English farmers who found Owen's restrictions on the brewing and drinking of ale vexatious and troubling to the spirit. Its name was the product of a code designed by one of its members which, to those who knew the code, revealed the exact latitude and longitude of the community.

Another source of dissent within the larger community included the vital question of whether the ideal commune should be rectangular or hexagonal in form. (Those of you who have attended a college faculty meeting will recognize the *genre*. Indeed, the famous "Boatload of Knowledge," carrying some of the leading scholars of the day, had followed closely behind Owen when he returned in January 1826. The makings of a faculty-type meeting were indeed present.)

Despite these minor defections and difficulties, Owen was encouraged enough, on July 4, 1826, to deliver his celebrated "Declaration of Mental Independence." I quote:

> I now declare to you and to the world, that Man, up to this hour, has been in all parts of the earth, a slave to a Trinity of the most monstrous evils that could be combined to inflict mental and physical evil upon his whole race. I refer to Private or Individual Property, Absurd and Irrational systems of Religion, and Marriage.

But as the oratory waxed, the economy of New Harmony waned. Agriculture, for example, was virtually at a standstill; the fences collapsed from want of repair, and the fields grew up in weeds. In desperation, on August 25, 1826, the people held a meeting at which they abolished all offices then existing and appointed three men as dictators.

On November 11, the *Gazette* carried a speech of Owen's in which he spoke in glowing terms of the progress of the community; but by January of 1827, Owen was selling property to individuals, the greater part of the town was resolved into individual lots; commercial enterprises took over most of the stores and sought a clientele with the vulgar signs of the capitalist heresy; a wax-figure and puppet show was opened at one end of the boarding house, and communalism as a way of life vanished as quickly as it had appeared.

In June of 1827, Owen took leave of New Harmony, never to return. Fortunately, he divided the land among his sons, who stayed on in Indiana and proved to be men of great spirit and intelligence, very real assets to the soon-to-be-state—but that's another story.

In 1842, a student of communalist societies by the name of Macdonald visited New Harmony and reported as follows:

> I was cautioned not to speak of Socialism, as the subject was unpopular. The advice was good; Socialism *was* unpopular, and with good reason. The people had been wearied and disappointed by it; had been filled with theories, until they were nauseated, and had made such miserable attempts at practice, that they seemed ashamed of

> what they had been doing. An enthusiastic socialist would soon be cooled down at New Harmony.

But not, of course, the dedicated utopian; thus John Humphrey Noyes, historian of American socialisms and one of the founders in the 1840s of the Oneida community in New York, closed his remarkably honest survey of the New Harmony experiment by saying that "we can still be sure that the *idea* of Owen and his thousand was not a delusion, but an inspiration, that only needed wiser hearts, to become a happy reality."[2] In other words, as with the modern socialisms (all of which, in my opinion, have been failures to the extent that they were socialist), the fault is never with the idea itself but always with its particular form of implementation.

It is with this idea that I take fundamental disagreement. I prefer to Noyes' evaluation of New Harmony that of a man identified only as L. Bolles and included in Noyes' section on New Harmony. I quote:

> The popular idea is that Owen and his class of reformers had an ideal that was very beautiful and very perfect; that they had too much faith for their time—too much faith in humanity; that they were several hundred years in advance of their age; and that the world was not good enough to understand them and their beautiful ideas. That is the

---

[2] John Humphrey Noyes, *History of American Socialisms* (1870), p. 43.

> superficial view of these men. I think the truth is, they were not up to the times; that mankind, in point of real faith, was ahead of them. Their view that the evils in human nature is owing to outward surroundings, is an impeachment of the providence of God. But they have taught us one great lesson; and that is that good circumstances do *not* make good men.[3]

In my view, the Robert Owen who showed the world the way to a better life for all was not the Owen of New Harmony but the Owen of New Lanark, the hard-headed businessman who proved that the humane treatment of others works, that is, it serves the purposes of both employer and employee. In my view, New Harmony should be seen, not as a monument to man's idealism, but as a testament to man's capacity to delude himself about his real nature.

[3] Ibid., pp. 54–55.

Part III

On the Nature of Economics

In this part on the nature of the economics, pride of place goes naturally to the paper on Adam Smith, the Father of Economics. This paper was first presented to an audience at Hillsdale College. In it, I make no attempt to conceal my opinion that Adam Smith is still the best of all of us who have labored in this particular vineyard.

The second paper in this section, "Christian Economics: Myth or Reality?" was written as an attempt to relate economics as a science to those questions of right and wrong policy that are the stuff of the real world. I accepted an invitation to present a paper at a Seminar on Economics and Ethics held at Valparaiso University in early 1965, and this paper is the result of that rash acceptance.

The third paper, "College Economics: Is It Subversive of Capitalism?" was presented to the Conservative Club at Yale University in the fall of 1967. Many of the older alumni of schools like Yale were convinced then (and now) that the members of the economics departments of their old colleges were ringleaders in the conspiracy to "do in" the capitalist system. In my paper. I argue that the very nature of economics is such as to make those fears largely groundless.

Chapter 1

Adam Smith: 1776-1976

"To prohibit a great people [the American colonials] . . . from making all that they can of every part of their own produce, or from employing their [capital] and industry in the way that they judge most advantageous to themselves, is a manifest violation of the most sacred rights of mankind." Adam Smith, *The Wealth of Nations*, 1776.

"We hold these truths to be self-evident, that all men are created equal, that they are endowed by their Creator with certain unalienable Rights, that among these are Life, Liberty, and the Pursuit of Happiness." Thomas Jefferson, "Declaration of Independence," 1776.

In these two passages we find one of the common elements in the two significant bicentennials we celebrate this year. That element is the conviction that man is endowed by a source greater than himself with certain natural and hence inalienable rights. This common element in the two bicentennials is one of the themes I shall develop in these comments of mine. But first let me hasten to admit that, in the households of the United States in 1976, the two bicentennials (the publication of *The Wealth of Nations* and the proclamation of the Declaration of Independence) are not held in equal awareness or veneration, nor does Adam Smith's name compete for the attention of the young with that of Thomas Jefferson. Yet it is my firm conviction that the members of our own society (and in fact of all societies based on the concept of freedom under law) must look to Smith as well as to Jefferson (and his fellow Founding Fathers) to fully understand our goodly heritage of freedom with order.

Here, as in all matters of judgment, I admit to bias. Adam Smith is generally known as the Father of Economics, the field of study which is also my own. Moreover, Smith's brand of economics, carrying the trademarks of voluntary exchange, freedom in the marketplace, and limited government, is also my brand of economics—Brand X though it may have become in today's intellectual marketplace. Finally, I believe Adam Smith not only to have been possessed of true wisdom about the nature and possibilities of the human condition but also to have been possessed of a capacity to communicate those ideas with great clarity and great style. In other words, I am an admitted, card-carrying Adam Smith buff.

With no embarrassment, I admit that I hope through these words to encourage some of you who may now know little of Smith and his work to come to want to know more. Even for those who bring to their studies of Smith a presupposition against his strong free-market policy position, there is something to be gained. His writing is free of that obscurantism, technical jargon, and complicated mathematics that distinguish most modern materials in economics. In Smith's writings, the case for what might be roughly called "capitalism" is put in so clear and straightforward a fashion that it makes a useful stone against which even the convinced socialist can hone his own counter-arguments. Finally, no one who professes to understand even commonly well the course of events of these last two hundred years can afford to be ignorant of the influence on that course of events of the ideas of Adam Smith, whether they have been proven right or wrong. In the words of the historian Henry Thomas Buckle, in his *The History of Civilization,* published in the middle of the last century: "In the year 1776, Adam Smith published his *Wealth of Nations,* which looking at its ultimate results, is probably the most important book that has ever been written." Even a true Smith buff may be at least mildly embarrassed by this claim, but that his ideas did have consequences, no one can really doubt (but more on this later).

Who was this man, what did he have to say in 1776, and how, if at all, is his thinking relevant to the world of 1976? Adam Smith was born in Kircaldy, Scotland, in 1723 and died in Edinburgh, Scotland, in 1790. In between he lived a life free of scandal, wife or children, great incident, and severe disappointment. He was a student (at Glasgow and Oxford), a teacher (at Glasgow and Edinburgh), and a scholar, and his friends were students, teachers and scholars—but also artists, writers, businessmen, and men of affairs. In a sense, though, he was the true "spectator" of the human scene, involved in that scene, yes, but always capable of detached analysis and appraisal of everything that came within his view.

My intent here is to concentrate on Smith's words and ideas and on their usefulness (if any) in interpreting the modern scene. Those of you who wish to know more of Smith's life or of the intellectual influences that shaped his thinking or of his weaknesses and strengths as a pure technician in the science of economics will need to look elsewhere.

My plan is as follows: First, to present in concise form what I see as Smith's view of the social order. Next, to identify the ways in which he applied this view to the world of his day, particularly the British treatment of the American colonies. Finally, to identify those ways in which it seems to me that Smith speaks most directly to the problems and possibilities of today's world.

Smith's Basic Argument

We begin with what I believe to be the essence of the Smith argument—but first a word of preparation.

The book whose bicentennial year we now celebrate has as its complete title, *An Inquiry into the Nature and Causes of the Wealth of Nations.*[1] The first sentence of Chapter I, Book I, reads as follows: "The greatest improvement in the productive powers of labour, and the greater part of the skill, dexterity, and judgment with which it is any where directed, or applied, seem to have been the effects of the division of labour." These substantial straws in the wind would seem to imply that we are about to grapple with a pure piece of economic analysis applied to the essentially vulgar question of how to multiply the quantity of "things" in a nation—and indeed Smith does have a kind word for those vulgar "things" when he writes, "No society can surely be flourishing and happy, of which the greater part of the members are poor and miserable."

But to see Smith as nothing more than an early-day consultant on how to make everyone rich is to do him an injustice. Smith was first and foremost a professor of moral philosophy, and his economic analysis was in a sense a byproduct of his concern with such questions as the nature of the universe, the nature of man, and the relationship of the individual to society.

When curiosity turns his attention to "the wealth of nations," he begins in effect by reaching into his philosopher's cupboard for the basic materials of his pro-

[1] Adam Smith, *The Wealth of Nations* (New York: Modern Library, 1937), p. 79.

posed studies. First and foremost he draws out his conviction that there exists a natural order in the universe which, if properly understood and lived in accordance with, tends to produce the "good." Coordinate with and deriving from this natural order is a set of natural rights of individuals (recall the phrasing of the opening passage from Smith—"the most sacred rights of mankind"). For a society to live in harmony with the natural order requires that it respect those "most sacred rights of mankind."

But what does all this have to do with getting more bread on the table? Comes now Smith, the eternal spectator, the observer of all that transpires around him, who is also curious as to what puts more bread on the table. His observations tell him very quickly that the wealth of a nation is primarily determined "by the skill, dexterity and judgment with which its labour is generally applied." But by what in turn are these determined? By two primary factors: (1) the extent to which the division of labor is carried in the society, and (2) the stock of capital available to the laborers.

But what forces give rise to or permit of the division of labor and the accumulation of capital? Must it be the forces of the ruler, commanding one man to do this and another to do that and ordering all to go without so that the stock of capital may grow? Not at all, replies Smith, the observer-philosopher. *In the natural order of things,* man is so disposed to act as to promote these very ends without the necessity of external commands.

The division of labor finds some part of its initial support in man's natural instinct to truck and barter. More importantly, the apparent problem of securing each man's cooperation in serving the needs of others proves to be no problem at all. His cooperation is readily secured, not out of his benevolence, but out of his natural regard for his own interest. "It is not from the benevolence of the butcher, the brewer, or the baker, that we expect our dinner, but from their regard to their own self-interest."

Thus the seeds of the division of labor lie in the very nature of man, that is, in the natural order. In the same way, man's desire for improvement induces him to save and hence to accumulate the capital needed to add even further to the productivity of labor.

But how are the activities of all of these specialists coordinated, what assures that the various parts and processes will be brought together properly in time and place and quantity and quality and all other relevant attributes? Surely here the offices of government must be required. Not at all, Smith replies; a spontaneous order emerges in the very nature of things, an order that arises out of the interaction in the marketplace between the two great forces of supply and demand.

If any one element in this complex chain comes to

be in short supply, its price will rise and suppliers will be induced to bring more to the market; in cases of excess supply, the reverse. In this way, in Smith's words, "the quantity of every commodity brought to market naturally suits itself to the effectual demand."[2]

The marketplace, then, as a spontaneously emerging and self-regulating process, is but the natural order at work in the ordering of economic life.

The pattern is now complete and he concludes as follows:

> As every individual, therefore, endeavours as much as he can both to employ his capital in the support of industry, and so to direct that industry that its produce may be of the greatest value; every individual necessarily labours to render the annual revenues of the society as great as he can. He generally indeed neither intends to promote the public interest, nor knows by how much he is promoting it. . . . [H]e intends only his own gain, and he is in this, as in many other cases, led by an invisible hand to promote an end which was no part of his intention.[3]

Continuing with Smith's words,

> All systems either of preference or of restraint, therefore, being thus completely taken away, the obvious and simple system of natural liberty establishes itself of its own accord. Every man, as long as he does not violate the laws of justice, is left perfectly free to pursue his own interest his

[2] Ibid., p. 57.

[3] Ibid., p. 423.

> own way, and to bring both his industry and capital into competition with those of any other man, or order of men. The sovereign is completely discharged from a duty, in the attempting to perform which he must always be exposed to innumerable delusions, and for the proper performance of which no human wisdom or knowledge could ever be sufficient; the duty of superintending the industry of private people, and of directing it towards the employments most suitable to the interest of the society. According to the system of natural liberty, the sovereign has only three duties to attend to; three duties of great importance, indeed, but plain and intelligible to common understandings: first, the duty of protecting the society from the violence and invasion of other independent societies; secondly, the duty of protecting, as far as possible, every member of the society from the injustice or oppression of every other member of it, or the duty of establishing an exact administration of justice; and, thirdly, the duty of erecting and maintaining certain public works and certain public institutions.[4]

Smith's Thinking Applied to the Problems of His Day

In a very real sense, *The Wealth of Nations* can be viewed as an attack on the prevailing economic philosophy and practice of the author's day—an untidy collection of ideas and actions identified as mercantilism. Mercantilism, as you know, was associated with the more powerful nation-states of seventeenth- and

[4] Ibid., p. 651.

eighteenth-century Europe, with England, France, Spain, Portugal, and Holland. Its primary purpose was to enhance the power and wealth of the nation, whether led by a king or a Cromwell or a parliament. The techniques were those of control—control not only of foreign trade (for the purpose of assuring a favorable balance of trade), control not only of colonies around the world, but control of most aspects of domestic economic life as well.

Smith argued that such controls were in fact directly opposed to the ultimate ends they were designed to serve. Thus, not only were the economic controls placed on her American colonies "a manifest violation of the most sacred rights of mankind," but moreover, "Under the present system of management Great Britain derives nothing but loss from the dominion which she assumes over her colonies."[5]

What were his proposals for the British colonies? Radical ones indeed! His first was "that Great Britain should voluntarily give up all authority over her colonies, and leave them to elect their own magistrates, to enact their own laws, and to make peace and war as they might think proper."[6] However, he admitted that this was "to propose such a measure as never was and never will be adopted, by any nation in the world." Why not? Not because such an action wouldn't be

[5] Ibid., p. 581.

[6] Ibid.

beneficial to the interests of the society but because it would be "mortifying to the pride" and because it would deprive the *rulers* "of the disposal of many places of trust and profit, of many opportunities of acquiring wealth and distinction, which the possession of the most turbulent, and, to the great body of the people, the most unprofitable province seldom fails to afford."[7]

His next and somewhat less sweeping proposal was that Great Britain give the colonies direct representation in Parliament. "Instead of piddling for the little prizes which are to be found in what may be called the paltry raffle of colony faction; they might then hope, from the presumption which men naturally have in their own ability and good fortune, to draw some of the great prizes which sometimes come from the wheel of the great state lottery of British politics."[8]

He goes on to argue that unless this or some other method is found of "preserving the importance and of gratifying the ambition of the leading men of America, it is not very probable that they will ever voluntarily submit to us." Moreover (in a phrase of shrewd prophecy), "They are very weak who flatter themselves that, in the state to which things have come, our colonies will be easily conquered by force alone."[9]

---

[7] Ibid., p. 582.

[8] Ibid., p. 587.

[9] Ibid.

"From shopkeepers, tradesmen, and attornies, they are become statesmen and legislators, and are employed in contriving a new form of government for an extensive empire, which, they flatter themselves, will become, and which, indeed, seems very likely to become, one of the greatest and most formidable that ever was in the world."[10]

These words could have been written no later than 1775 and speak well, at the very least, of Smith's powers of prophecy.

In concluding this section, I wish to point out that Smith's handling of the colonial question was in full accord with and, in fact, derived directly from his general philosophy of free peoples, free economies, and free societies.

Is Smith Still Relevant?

The question now before us is whether Smith's work is of only antiquarian interest to those of us who inhabit the world of 1976—or does it have some continuing relevance? I intend to argue that Smith does indeed provide us with most useful insights into our own problems and with those insights often so phrased as to make them at least the equal in power of persuasion of any later versions of the same think-

[10] Ibid., pp. 587–88.

ing. I offer up now for your examination a series of examples, presented in no particular order.

To those who call for the businessman (or others) to act less on self-interest and more on the desire to serve others, he answers: "I have never known much good done by those who affected to trade for the public good. It is an affectation, indeed, not very common among merchants, and very few words need be employed in dissuading them from it."[11]

To those who are now calling for some kind of national economic plan for the United States, he responds:

> What is the species of domestic industry which his capital can employ, and of which the produce is likely to be of the greatest value, every individual, it is evident, can, in his local situation, judge much better than any statesman or lawgiver can do for him. The statesman, who should attempt to direct private people in what manner they ought to employ their capitals, would not only load himself with a most unnecessary attention, but assume an authority which could safely be trusted, not only to no single person, but to no council or senate whatever, and which would nowhere be so dangerous as in the hands of a man who had folly and presumption enough to fancy himself fit to exercise it.[12]

To those special interests who demand protection from goods produced in other countries: "By means

[11] Ibid., p. 423.

[12] Ibid.

of glasses, hotbeds and hotwalls, very good grapes can be raised in Scotland, and very good wines too can be made of them *at about thirty times the expense* from which at least equally good can be brought from foreign countries. Would it be a reasonable law to prohibit the importation of all foreign wines, merely to encourage the making of claret and burgundy in Scotland?"[13]

To the tendency of governors and governments to reduce the purchasing power of the money (that is, to produce inflation):

> In every country of the world, I believe, the avarice and injustice of princes and sovereign states, abusing the confidence of their subjects, have by degrees diminished the real quantity of metal, which had been originally contained in their coins. The Roman As, in the latter ages of the Republic, was reduced to the twenty-fourth part of its original value. . . . The English pound and penny contain at present about a third only; the Scots pound and penny about a thirty-sixth; and the French pound and penny about a sixty-sixth part of their original value. . . . Such operations have always proved favorable to the debtor, and ruinous to the creditor, and have sometimes produced a greater and more universal revolution in the fortunes of private persons, than could have been occasioned by a very great public calamity.[14]

On the behavior of organizations of workers: "Their usual pretences are sometimes the high price of pro-

---

[13] Ibid., p. 425.

[14] Ibid., pp. 27–28.

visions; sometimes the great profit which their masters make by their work . . . . [T]heir combinations . . . are always abundantly heard of. In order to bring the point to a speedy decision, they have always recourse to the loudest clamour, and sometimes to the most shocking violence and outrage."[15]

In fact, though, Smith's sympathies were with the workers (as against the masters), and he was pleased with what he observed to be the improvement in the lot of the common worker in the England of his day. "The common complaint that luxury extends itself even to the lowest ranks of the people, and that the labouring poor will not now be contented with the same food, clothing and lodging which satisfied them in former times, may convince us that it is not the money price of labour only, but its real recompence which has augmented."[16]

To the argument that the workman (and those who use his services) must be protected by apprenticeships, licensing, wage-setting by law or what-have-you, he responds:

> The property which every man has in his own labour, as it is the original foundation of all other property, so it is the most sacred and inviolable. The patrimony of a poor man lies in the strength and dexterity of his hands; but to hinder him from employing this strength and dexterity in what manner he thinks proper without injury to his

[15] Ibid., p. 67.

[16] Ibid., p. 78.

> neighbour, is a plain violation of this most sacred property. It is a manifest encroachment upon the just liberty both of the workman, and of those who might be disposed to employ him. As it hinders the one from working at what he thinks proper, so it hinders the others from employing whom they think proper. To judge whether he is fit to be employed, may surely be trusted to the discretion of the employers whose interest it so much concerns.[17]

But his criticism of some practices of workmen should not be taken to mean that he was uncritical of the businessman or merchant. To many of both the initiated and the uninitiated, Adam Smith is seen as a spokesman for the business interest. Thus, for reasons that can only be guessed at, when the Modern Library edition of *The Wealth of Nations* was published in 1937, it included an introduction by Max Lerner, then editor of *The Nation*.

In his introduction, Lerner writes that Smith "was an unconscious mercenary in the service of a rising capitalist class . . . . [H]e gave a new dignity to greed and a new sanctification of the predatory impulses . . . . [H]e rationalized the economic interests of the class that was coming to power."[18]

Even though Lerner admits that "Smith's doctrine has been twisted in ways he would not have approved," the damage is already done, and Smith is confirmed again in the mind of the reading public as the puppet

---

[17] Ibid., pp. 121–22.

[18] Ibid., pp. ix–x.

of the bourgeois business interest—a view of him that continues to this day to color the thinking of those who might otherwise learn from him.

Compare this view of Smith with these words in which he describes the proper attitude of the society to proposals for legislation coming from businessmen (and which serves equally well to answer those today who believe that we can best solve our problems by turning over our economic decision-making to good, experienced, competent leaders of business): "The proposal of any new law or regulation which comes from this order [the businessmen] ought always to be listened to with great precaution, and ought never to be adopted till after having been long and carefully examined, not only with the most scrupulous, but with the most suspicious attention."[19]

Nor is Smith at all unaware of the ancient (and modern) propensity of businessmen (as well as others) to attempt to combine to restrict competition. In a famous passage he writes that "People of the same trade seldom meet together, even for merriment and diversion, but the conversation ends in a conspiracy against the public, or in some contrivance to raise prices."[20]

At the same time, his recommendations for dealing with such cases seem to me to reflect greater wisdom

---

[19] Ibid., p. 250.

[20] Ibid., p. 128.

than our policies of today. He continues from the statement above: "It is impossible indeed to prevent such meetings, by any law which either could be executed, or would be consistent with liberty and justice. But though the law cannot hinder people of the same trade from sometimes assembling together, it ought to do nothing to facilitate such assemblies; much less to render them necessary."[21]

But wouldn't such a policy leave the public to the none-too-tender mercies of the conspirators? Not at all, replies Smith. Why not? Because in the absence of government backing, such conspiracies do not survive. "In a free trade an effectual combination cannot be established but by the unanimous consent of every single trader, and it cannot last longer than every single trader continues of the same mind. The majority of a corporation [i.e., of a government-granted monopoly power to a group of traders] can enact a by-law with proper penalties, which will limit the competition more effectually and more durably than any voluntary combination whatever."[22]

As a matter of fact, in this whole area of competition and monopoly, it seems to me that Smith speaks with more wisdom than most modern economists and most of the associated legislation. Smith creates no

---

[21] Ibid.

[22] Ibid., p. 129.

unattainable ideal of "perfect competition" as a bench mark for use in appraisal and policy-making. Rather he argues that "all systems either of preference or of restraint . . . being thus completely taken away"—that is, all government interventionist action removed from the marketplace—"the obvious and simple system of natural liberty establishes itself of its own accord."[23]

In other words, all that governments must do to see that competition (i.e., the open marketplace) prevails is *not* to create monopoly. Competition does not need to be created or protected or restored—it inheres in the natural order of things and in the very nature of man. I believe this to have been true in 1776 and to be equally true in 1976. The technological changes of the last two hundred years have served only to make the competitive process *more* intense and to ensure the even quicker demise of the firm that doesn't maintain a perpetual effort to serve its customers better.

But enough of the examples. If you are not yet persuaded of Smth's continuing relevance, a further parade of cases is not likely to be useful. God knows I may be in error, but I am convinced that Smith is not only relevant today but that his insight and wisdom, if applied to today's world, would yield not only a freer but a more productive and equitable set of economic arrangements than if we applied a mixture of

[23] Ibid., p. 651.

what was thought to be the best of contemporary thought.

This does not mean that I have no quarrels with Smith; his third function of government seems to me to be a Pandora's box; his handling of the theory of value, of what determines the ratio of exchange among goods and services, seems to me to be importantly in error, etc.

At the same time, I yield to no one in my admiration for his wisdom and for his magnificant contribution to our understanding of ourselves and of our institutions, in the form particularly of this book whose bicentenary year of publication we celebrate this year. It was from this book that such disparate types as William Pitt and Edmund Burke in England and Alexander Hamilton and John Adams in this country admitted having drawn some part of their own thinking on political economy. It is my reasoned conviction that the well-being of every society in the modern world would be at a significantly higher level if more of those in leadership roles in our societies of today were to be reading *The Wealth of Nations* rather than the modern works from which they draw their tragically mistaken policy advice.

I close now with a final offering of the wisdom of Adam Smith, this on the inherent error in *all* systems of control and this one coming not from *The Wealth of Nations* but from his first book, *The Theory of Moral Sentiments.*

The man of system, is apt to be very wise in his own conceit, and is often so enamoured with the supposed beauty of his own ideal plan of government, that he cannot suffer the smallest deviation from any part of it. He goes on to establish it completely and in all its parts, without any regard either to the great interests or to the strong prejudices which may oppose it: he seems to imagine that he can arrange the different members of a great society with as much ease as the hand arranges the different pieces upon a chess-board; he does not consider that the pieces upon the chess-board have no other principle of motion besides that which the hand impresses upon them; but that, in the great chess-board of human society, every single piece has a principle of motion of its own, altogether different from that which the legislature might choose to impress upon it. If those two principles coincide and act in the same direction, the game of human society will go on easily and harmoniously, and is very likely to be happy and successful. If they are opposite or different, the game will go on miserably, and the society must be at all times in the highest degree of disorder.

Chapter 2

Christian Economics: Myth or Reality?

I wish to begin my discussion with some questions. What can we find in the Bible on the ethical rightness of the statement that two plus two equals four? What do the Papal Encyclicals tell us of the justice of Boyle's Law, that the volume of an ideal gas varies inversely with its pressure, other things being equal? Does Christian doctrine tell us that it is fair for a hydrogen atom to contain three isotopes while a fluorine atom contains but two? Or, to approach my own topic, is it Christian or un-Christian for a demand curve to be negatively inclined from left to right?

Economics as a Pure Science

Let me now put the general case: What does Christianity have to do with the questions of any pure science? So that there can be no suspense, I shall give the answer immediately. The answer is, "Nothing, absolutely nothing." There can no more be a Christian science of economics than there can be a Christian science of mathematics. It was a Hindu who first introduced zero into the set of real numbers and a Greek pagan who first analyzed the process of exchange in the marketplace. A microscope and a telescope seem to be quite indifferent to the religion of those who peer through them. The law of diminishing returns has no more relationship to the flight from Egypt than it does to the flight from Mecca to Medina.

Am I belaboring my point unnecessarily? Perhaps not. The proponents of all of the world's great religions, including Christianity, have often yielded to the temptation of dictating answers to particular questions of pure science—and have always been made to appear foolish in the process. Is the earth round or flat? Is the earth the center of the universe or isn't it? Was the world created at 9:00 on the morning of October 23rd, 4,004 B.C.? And, as Clarence Darrow asked, was that Central Standard Time or Mountain Standard Time? And as the quasi-religionists of modern communism ask, cannot acquired characteristics be inherited? I would be belaboring my point if it were not for the likelihood that many a scientist may yet be forced to kneel in the snow outside the temple and beg forgiveness for the impertinence of his findings.

If economics were *only* a pure science, we could now consider my presentation at an end and say, if all were to agree with me, that Christian economics is indeed a myth and a most unnecessary one at that. But economics is both something less and something more than a pure science, and therein lies the rub.

Economics as Something Less than a Pure Science

Let me begin with the implications of the fact that economics is something less than a pure science—but first let me define what I mean by a pure science. A pure science is one that is concerned with *what is* and not with what *should be*. I shall refer to economics as a pure science as *positive* economics and to economics as a set of do's and don'ts as *normative* economics.

Now economics is something less than a pure science only in a special sense. Its goal of finding out "what is" is no different from that of physics or astronomy, and economists often use search methods quite like those used by the natural scientists. What makes economics something less than a pure science is its present lack of success in developing a body of laws or generalizations accepted as correct by all or almost all serious students of the subject. The state of economics today is not unlike the state of physics at the time of Galileo's recantation.

Even at the level of what is, economists are so far short of agreement on so many fundamental questions that the well-intentioned layman can almost always find some economist who will provide him with scientific evidence of the correctness of what he *wants* to believe to be true.

Let me illustrate: The question of whether a minimum wage set by government does or does not increase the total wage payments going to a given group of workers is a question in positive economics. Yet in appearances before ministers, I have been accused of being un-Christian because *my* findings are that the long-run effect of a minimum wage is to *reduce* the total income of the workers involved.

Nor can I really be angry at this. The ministers involved want very much to believe that the problem of poverty can be solved in part by simply passing a law increasing hourly wage rates—and they can find economists of more repute than Ben Rogge who will tell them that this can, in fact, be done. When the scientists disagree, the layman is going to choose the scientist who tells him what he wants to hear.

What does the fact that economics is still itself an underdeveloped area mean to the Christian? If it is the economist who himself is also a Christian, it seems to me to require of him an open mind, integrity in dealing with his own findings and the findings of others, and a refusal to let his wishes be father to his facts.

When the great English historian Herbert Butterfield visited the Wabash campus a few years ago, he was asked if there was such a thing as Christian history. He replied that there wasn't, but that there was history *as written by a Christian* and that the man's Christianity would demand of him that he display the attitudes I have just described.

But what does the incomplete and confused state of economic science mean to the Christian who is not a professional economist but who wishes to use economic knowledge in making his own decisions? It seems to me that it requires of him the same openness of mind, the same refusal to let his wishes be father to his facts that it requires of the economist. He ought to be anxious to expose himself to various sources of economic information and to learn from them all that he can. Economic science may be in a primitive state, but this is only relative to some of the more mature sciences, and it still has much to teach the typical nonprofessional.

I will say flatly that the typical American who calls himself a Christian, and who makes pronouncements or joins in making pronouncements on economic policies or institutions, does so out of an almost complete ignorance of the simplest and most widely accepted tools of economic analysis. If something arouses his Christian concern, he asks not whether it is water or gasoline he is tossing on the economic fire—he asks only whether it is a well-intended act. As I understand it, the Christian is required to be something more than well-meaning; he is required to use his God-given reason as well. Inadequate as economic science may now be, it can save the layman from at least the grossest errors and can be ignored only at real peril to the society at large.

Let me summarize my thesis up to this point: I have argued that the word *Christian* is totally out of place as a modifier to any of the pure sciences. Generically, economics is one of the pure sciences and hence this constraint must apply to the concept of Christian economics. The main thrust of this constraint is undisturbed by the fact that economics is still in a primitive state of development. However, this fact requires of the Christian, whether a professional economist or no, a certain caution, a certain openness to various possibilities not required (at least to the same degree) in dealing with the laws of the more precise and more mature sciences. But this fact does not excuse anyone, be he Christian or no, from the necessity of learning what he can about economics before making decisions on economic policy.

Economics as Something More than a Pure Science

This brings me to the second part of my discussion, to the implications of the fact that economics is something *more* than a pure science. There is a *positive* economics but there is also a *normative* economics—an economics that is concerned with questions of valuaation, of right and wrong action or inaction. I have denied that there can be a Christian positive economics; let me now ask if there can be a Christian normative economics.

Normative economics is positive economics plus a value system. Christianity is a religion, and a religion need not involve a set of values—but, of course, Christianity does. It follows that the value system in the normative economics of a Christian should be the Christian value system. *In this sense, then, Christian economics can be very much of a reality.* It will be marked, not by its choice of materials from positive economics, but by its choice of fundamental assumptions about the nature of man, his purposes here on earth, and the obligations for right action imposed upon him by his Creator. I assume that these fundamental assumptions would be drawn from what the Christian believes to be the revealed word of God, that is, from the Bible and from such interpretations of the Bible as the particular Christian accepts as authoritative.

So far, so good; but as an economist embarrassed by the relative chaos in his own field, I cannot resist pointing out that there seems to be more than one value system labeled "Christian." Perhaps I should rephrase my earlier affirmation and say that not only can there be a Christian economics, there can be *any number* of Christian economics. However, I don't wish to disturb the state of happy (though perhaps superficial) ecumenism in which we seem to be basking at this time in

America, and so I shall concentrate on what seem to me to be the least controversial, the most widely agreed-upon precepts of Christianity.

What I want to do now is to list a number of these precepts and then keep them in mind as I examine just one specific question in normative economics. If there is, indeed, a Christian normative economics (as I am arguing there is), we should be able to use it, should we not? My real purpose in doing this is not to provide you with an answer to this one question but to reveal some of the dilemmas the Christian encounters in applying Christian values to problems of economic policy.

In listing these precepts, I make no claim for completeness or absolutely universal acceptance by all Christians. I list them as the ones that seem to me and (to the best of my knowledge) to others as the ones most relevant to social problems.

Some Basic Assumptions

I begin with the assumption that *man is imperfect,* now and forever—that he is, indeed, somewhat lower than the angels. It follows that all of his constructs must be imperfect; William Blake and the Anglican hymnal to the contrary, Jerusalem is never to be built in England's green and pleasant land.

Next I place on the list the Christian view of *man as*

a responsible being. In the words of John Bennett of Union Theological Seminary,

> Man never ceases to be a responsible being and no mere victim of circumstance or of the consequences of the sins of his fathers. Man has the amazing capacity through memory and thought and imagination to transcend himself and his own time and place, to criticize himself and his environment on the basis of ideals and purposes that are present to his mind, and he can aspire in the grimmest situation to realize these ideals and purposes in his personal life and in society. In is this capacity for self-transcendence that Reinhold Niebuhr, following Augustine, regards as the chief mark of the image of God in man that is never lost.[1]

My third of the Christian assumptions is that of the significance of man's *freedom to choose.* In its most elemental form, this signifies Christ's insistence that he wanted as followers, only those who had freely chosen him and his way. I remind you of one of the most dramatic scenes in literature, the challenging of Christ by the Grand Inquisitor in *The Brothers Karamazov.* I shall argue in a moment that this Christian sense of freedom is a most annoying restraint on social action and, hence, is the one precept most commonly ignored in Christian communities.

Next and very important is the assumption of *the*

[1] John C. Bennett, *Christianity and Communism Today* (1960), p. 118.

brotherhood of man, with its clear implication of the necessity of assisting those in need. The crucial importance of this assumption in the drafting of Christian economic policy can hardly be overemphasized.

I now add one of the explicit guidelines (and another very annoying restraint on social action), *Thou shalt not steal.*

I close the list with the Christian's sense of the forgiving love of God and of the ultimate hope that comes with the knowledge that this is God's world. John Bennett, in discussing this sense in conjunction with a discussion of man's sin, puts it this way:

> Christian teaching about human nature perhaps reveals most clearly the corrective elements in Christianity. It corrects all tendencies toward sentimental optimism or utopianism that fail to prepare men to face the stubborn reality of evil in human history, and it corrects all tendencies to disillusionment or cynicism that are the opposite danger. Men who lack the perspective of Christian teaching are in danger of oscillating between utopianism and disillusionment.
>
> The first thing that Christians say about human nature is that man—and this means every man—is made in the image of God and that this image is the basis of man's dignity and promise.
>
> The second thing that Christians say about human nature is that man—and this means every man and not merely those who are opponents or enemies—is a sinner.[2]

[2] Ibid., pp. 116–17.

Christian Economics: A Case Study

My choice of precepts to include may have already cost me your good will, but now that we have the list, good, bad, or indifferent, let us see if we can put it to work.

Here is our problem: A family in (say) Valparaiso, Indiana, lives in serious poverty, with not always enough money for food, clothing for the children, medicine or doctor's services, or for rent on their small, ramshackle house. What does Christian economics tell us to do about this? What kind of a war on poverty does it ask us to wage?

Let us turn first to the kind of answer usually given by the American society generally today (and also the kind of answer generally endorsed by the social action groups of the large denominational organizations and of the National Council of Churches).

First, we should pass a law called a minimum wage law to force this man's employer to pay him a living wage. Or we should encourage the development of a union in this man's work group so that he could expect to receive a fair and decent wage. Next, we ought to pass laws that will force such men to save for emergencies, for example, unemployment, which may be the man's real problem at the moment. If he is unemployed, the government should offer him subsidized retraining, so that he can find suitable employment. If he is in real need, as our particular man is at the moment, some combination of local, state, and national relief payments should be made to him.

This is what most Christians in America today deem appropriate, with perhaps the addition of a box of groceries collected by one of the churches to be delivered to the family each Thanksgiving and Christmas.

Does any of this lack good intent? I think not; on the surface, at least, it seems to meet the requirement imposed by the brotherhood of man.

Minimum Wages

Now let's go through it again to see if we've missed anything. We begin with the idea of a legislated increase in his wage rate. Perhaps it would be wise if we first asked what the consequences of this might be. For example, could it lead to this man's losing his job altogether, either immediately or as the employer is forced by the higher costs of labor to mechanize the operation, if he is to stay in business at all? Well, says the economist, that will depend in part on whether the labor market was competitive to begin with, whether the man was already getting all that he was really worth. It will depend on whether this law "jars" the employer into becoming more efficient. In other words, it will depend on a number of factors of the kind analyzed in positive economics.

My own personal knowledge both of theory and of

evidence would lead me to argue that the very probable consequence of a legislated increase in wage rates will be some loss of employment opportunities, and our particular worker could well be one of those to lose his job. I might add that his chances of being thrown out of work are increased if he is a member of a minority racial group.

I may be wrong on this, but I know of no competent economist who would deny the possibility that a legislated minimum wage will produce some unemployment. If this possibility exists, a Christian might well wish to examine the findings of positive economics before supporting a proposal of this kind. In supporting the idea of minimum wage laws, the Christian may well be causing problems for precisely those people he wishes to help, and be giving aid and comfort to a more fortunate worker-employer group which benefits by being freed of the competition of lower-wage firms. I repeat, good Christian intentions are not enough!

Trade Unions

Similar questions might well be raised about the second line of attack on our special problem of poverty —that of encouraging the development of a trade union to protect this worker. A union-induced increase in wage rates in the plant or store where this man works could lead to his losing his job altogether, just as in the other case. If he is a member of a minority race, the chances of this will be even higher under the trade union approach, because of the long-established discriminatory practices of many of the important unions. For example, in 1962, there were only three Negro apprentices in the union-dominated electrical trade in all of New York City and only one Negro apprentice plumber.

Here again the Ben Rogge version of positive economics could be wrong, but again the important questions are those of positive economics and not of good intent.

At least one additional question might be raised. In granting special privileges, immunities, and encouragement to trade unions, we would be sanctioning any activity that when undertaken by businessmen can lead to their being put in jail. As an economic institution (and a trade union is more than an economic institution), a union is a cartel; that is, it is a collusive arrangement among otherwise independent sellers of the services of labor, for the purpose of manipulating market prices to their own advantage. It is precisely the same in operation as the activities of the sales executives of the large electrical manufacturing companies that led to their being sent to prison a year or two ago. In encouraging workers (and farmers) to do that which we forbid businessmen, we seem to be violating a rather old concept of justice—that of equality before the law. To encourage trade unionism may be wise or unwise economic policy but surely the Christian cannot escape some concern for a policy that deliberately creates a double standard of right and wrong.

Social Security

We turn now to the third of the responses to our problem, that of social security. Let us force such people to contribute to a program to tide them over such emergencies. This may be wise or unwise economic policy, but at least it will assure some minimal flow of income to the family for some period of time. In other words, it does work.

Some Christians might be disturbed to know that as the system now works in this country, low-income Negroes are being taxed to support high-income whites. How does this come about? A low-income but fully employed Negro will pay into the fund almost as much money as will the high-income white. But the average life span of the Negro beyond age 65 is significantly less than that of the white, and the Negro can thus expect to draw less in total benefits. I present this odd circumstance, not as a criticism of social security *per se,* because the law could be changed to eliminate this feature, but as further evidence of the need for the well-intentioned person to examine policy proposals, not only in the large, but in detail as well.

But clearly, within certain limits, social security

does work; it does provide much needed help to many in real need.

Surely the Christian can find no dilemma here. *No?* What, then, of the Mennonites and the Amish who have fiercely resisted any participation in this program? Of course, these are patently queer people, who wear funny-looking clothes and have other peculiar ideas, but they *do* call themselves Christians; in fact, they say that it is *because* they are Christians that they must refuse to involve themselves in social security.

How could this possibly be? Let us go back to our precepts of religion and see what we can find. Suppose we interpret the brotherhood of man, individual responsibility, and freedom to choose as meaning that each man should be free to choose, even in economic life; that if he chooses wrongly he is responsible and should seek himself to solve the problems he has created for himself; and that, if this proves impossible, it then becomes the responsibility of his fellow Christians, *as a voluntary act of brotherhood,* to come to his assistance. Surely, this line of reasoning cannot be immediately labeled as un-Christian—even if it would confront us with the embarrassing challenge of doing something individually, directly, and out of our own pockets for this family in Valparaiso, Indiana, of which we have personal knowledge.

Take "freedom to choose." Does this apply only in questions of pure religion, or does it constitute a general Christian presumption in favor of freedom of the individual? If the latter, then the Christian faces a dilemma. Social security tells a man that he must pay into the fund, how much he must pay at a minimum, and in what form the fund will be held. Whether on balance this is good or bad, it is clearly a denial of freedom. In the words of the English philosopher, Isaiah Berlin, in discussing this general type of dilemma:

> A sacrifice is not an increase in what is being sacrificed, namely freedom, however great the moral need or the compensation for it. Everything is what it is: liberty is liberty, not equality or fairness or justice or human happiness or a quiet conscience. . . . This [loss] may be compensated for by a gain in justice or in happiness or in peace, but the loss remains, and it is nothing but a confusion of values to say that although my "liberal," individual freedom may go by the board, some other kind of freedom—"social" or "economic"—is increased.[3]

Here then is a typical dilemma of the Christian as he approaches economic policy; his concern for his brother leads him to favor a measure that will help his brother (such as social security) but, to be really effective, it requires that he also reduce his brother's freedom to choose. I note, somewhat sadly, that given this choice, the majority of Christian peoples have usually chosen to sacrifice their own freedom and the freedom of others in the interest of compelling people to do what all good Christians know they should do. This

[3] Isaiah Berlin, *Two Concepts of Liberty* (1958), p. 10.

may or may not be the right decision on the question of social security, but let no Christian say yes, it *is* the right decision, with a feeling that no sacrifice of any principle is involved.

Redistribution of Income

The last two approaches, retraining the worker and providing him with direct relief, are but two forms of the same thing and I shall treat them as a unit. Government-provided relief is a forced redistribution of income from one group of people to another group of people. Subsidized retraining is simply a form of redistributive payment that the beneficiary can receive only if he takes it in a given form, that is, in the form of tuition-free schooling, combined with subsistence payments. Whether redistribution is more efficient if the uses of the money by the beneficiaries are directed by the government (as in retraining programs, government housing, school lunch provisions, and the like) than if the money is simply turned over to the beneficiaries to be used as they wish, is a complex question and one that I don't have time to examine. I would point out only that he who pays the piper, whether he be private person or a government agent, will usually be strongly tempted to call the tune. In other words, as a matter of sociological probability, most schemes for redistributing income will usually involve some directing of the uses to which the beneficiaries may put the funds.

Whatever form the payments may take, relief provided by the state *does* work; it *does* provide assistance to the needy. It *does* provide food for the hungry, clothing and shelter for the cold, and medicine for the sick. Surely, here at last the Christian can relax, secure in the knowledge that in supporting such measures he is recognizing the obligations imposed upon him by the fact of human brotherhood in God.

Perhaps—but perhaps not. As I understand it, these obligations rest upon each individual to be acted upon as a matter of conscience. As I remember the parable, the Good Samaritan was not acting upon an order of government in performing his good deed, nor was he a paid official of a local welfare agency, drawing on local tax funds. Does Christian virtue consist in passing a law to force oneself to do what is charitable and right? Given man's imperfect nature, this might be a tenable position. Unfortunately, though, the law must apply to all; and thus many, who, for whatever reason, do not *wish* to give up what is theirs for the use of others, are physically compelled to do so.

Under Which Christian Precept Can Force Be Justified?

Ah, but you say, they *should* wish to do so. Of course they should, but if they don't, is the Christian then authorized to use force to compel them to do so? If so, under which of the precepts of Christianity?

Aquinas apparently had found such a precept when he wrote, "The superfluities of the rich belong by right to the poor. . . . To use the property of another, taking it secretly in case of extreme need, cannot, properly speaking, be characterized as theft."[4] Others might be troubled, though, by the apparent conflict between this interpretation and the commandment, Thou shalt not steal. Perhaps it should read, Thou shalt not steal, except to give to the poor. Under this interpretation, King Ahab and Jezebel would have been justified in seizing Naboth's vineyard, if their purpose had been to distribute its fruits among the poor.

It is interesting to note the way in which these questions are handled in the thirty-eighth of the Articles of Religion of the Protestant Episcopal Church in the United States:

> The Riches and Goods of Christians are not common, as touching the right, title, and possession of the same; as certain Anabaptists do falsely boast. Notwithstanding, every man ought, of such things as he possesseth, liberally give alms to the poor, according to his ability.

It would seem possible to develop what might be called a Christian position on this issue that would strike against *all* public charity and make assistance to

---

[4] Thomas Aquinas, *Summa Theologica,* 2a, 2ae, quaestiao 66, art. 7.

the needy a response of the individual conscience. This is in fact a position taken by certain denominational groups in the country today.

The Personal Practice of Freedom

Am I really saying that I think the vast responsibilities for assistance to the needy in our modern, complex society could be entrusted to private individuals and voluntary welfare agencies; do I really think that, under such a system, no one would be left out, no child would ever die of hunger or cold? I honestly don't know *what* the consequences would be of such an arrangement. I only know that the Christian who enthusiastically embraces coercive, collective charity may very possibly be deriving his mandate from some source other than his own religion. For example, such an approach fits very well with a psychological interpretation of man as a helpless victim of his environment, as a creature not to be held responsible for his own successes or failures. If you answer the question, "Who's to blame?" not with "Mea Culpa," but with "Society," you need not hesitate to turn to the central agency of organized society, the state, to solve any and all problems.

It is of course as presumptuous of me to talk of Christian doctrine as it might be for some of you to talk of technical economics; but I must confess that my own personal interpretation of Christianity does not fit well with most of the approaches to social and economic problems of official Christendom in this country today. *Today's Christian economics seems to me to be neither good Christianity nor good economics.*

But my function here is not to offer you advice on what to accept and what to reject. That I have done so, both directly and by implication, lends further credence to the thesis of one of my favorite modern philosophers, Charlie Brown of the *Peanuts* comic strip, who was once led to remark, "This world is filled with people who are anxious to function in an advisory capacity."

If Economists Disagree, Let Christians Be Tolerant

My function here has been to discuss the topic, "Christian Economics; Myth or Reality?" I have argued that the word *Christian* cannot and must not be used as a modifier to economics as a pure science. To do so is to indulge in the ancient sin of trying by appeal to revelation to answer certain questions that were meant to be answered by man himself with the use of his God-given reason.

I have argued as well that, in spite of its present state of imperfection, economics as a pure science, that is, positive economics, has much to offer to those who are interested in questions of economic policy. As a matter of fact, I think myself that *much of the diversity of opinion among economists, both amateur and professional, on questions of public policy stems not from disagreement over ultimate goals or values but from disagreement over the findings of positive economics.* In a sense this is encouraging, because it implies that these disagreements can be reduced over time by improvement in the science itself. Disagreements over ultimate values cannot be resolved; they can only be fought over or ignored. Disagreements over questions of fact and analysis are conceptually open to solution.

I have also argued that there *can* be a Christian economics at the normative level; the Christian can combine his Christian ethics and Christian assumptions about the nature of man with his knowledge of positive economics to decide whether any given proposal should be approved or condemned. The combination can very properly be called Christian economics.

Unfortunately, because of disagreements at the level of *which* positive economics to accept and at the level of *which* interpretation of Christian values to accept, *there is no single set of conclusions on economic policy that can be said to be the definitive and unique Christian economics.* The socialist and the free enterpriser, the interventionist and the noninterventionist, the business spokesman and the labor spokesman, the Mennonite farmer and the Episcopalian President of the United States, Ben Rogge and John Kenneth Galbraith—each will argue that *his* answers are the ones most nearly in accord with *true* Christian economics. In this lies the challenge to the Christian.

The only advice I can offer the now thoroughly confused Christian is that he avoid hasty judgment and that he think with his head as well as with his heart. He must learn what he can from positive economics and carefully examine precisely what values are imposed upon him by the fact that he is a Christian. In the meantime, he can draw some comfort from the knowledge that the professional economists and the ministers of the Christian churches are but little less confused than he.

Chapter 3

College Economics: Is It Subversive of Capitalism?

So that you will not be left in suspense, let me tell you immediately that the amount of subversion that takes place in college economics courses is probably much less than you may have imagined. The reasons for this are many; two of the most important are as follows:

(1) In general, the level of teaching in economics (and particularly in the introductory course, which is the *only* formal course in economics taken by most American students—if they take even that) is generally of such poor quality that the students are neither subverted nor enlightened—primarily, they are *bored!*

(2) The second reason that less subversion by the left takes place in America college courses in economics than you may have imagined is that the student in these courses is *exposed* to less purely leftist economics than you may have imagined. But don't be too encouraged by this. Where the student *does* encounter

the true economic nonsense of the left is in his courses in literature, history, political science, social psychology, sociology (one of the worst offenders), and philosophy. The degree of certainty of this exposure to economic nonsense becomes almost absolute if he goes on to study to be a minister, a priest, or a rabbi.

I intend to concentrate on the introductory course, not only because it is the one taken by the largest number of students, but also because it reflects as well what happens in almost all of the advanced courses that follow it. Obviously I will be painting with a broad brush, and my comments will not be a description of each and every introductory course in economics in America nor of each and every teacher of such a course.

Let me begin by describing the organization of the typical introductory course in economics at an American university. (I might note that this description would apply equally well to the introductory course in almost any discipline or subject in the university.)

The director of the course will be a middle-level member of the department who has already been marked as a nonproducer; i.e., as a man who is not likely to bring fame to the department by his creative scholarship (or by what passes for it in most of the social sciences). His staff will consist largely of the several dozen graduate students and young instructors in economics who have not been able to secure research grants for the year; supplemented by a few regular members of the department who are told that they must teach in the introductory course at least once every fourth term; supplemented in turn by lectures delivered on occasion by some of the Big Names in the department—whose lectures must be fitted into their schedules of shorter or longer stays in Washington, D.C., at the U.N., or in Thailand.

Two or three times each week, the thousand or so students will gather in the largest auditorium on campus to hear lectures delivered by the director or one of his peripatetic stars; once or twice each week the students will meet in small quiz sessions, led by the young graduate students, who have nothing to gain by doing the job well and everything to lose if they spend so much time on their teaching as to fall behind in their graduate courses or their research for the doctoral dissertation. I speak from several years of direct personal experience in this role.

Assignments are made in a textbook, chosen usually from the list of "in" books—Samuelson, Reynolds, Bach, McConnell, etc. I might note that a really popular textbook can bring a Samuelson (say) as much money as Keynes made in speculating on the international money market, if not as much as Ricardo made in speculating in government consols at the time of the Battle of Waterloo. Students are also given assignments in workbooks, computing demand elasticities or deflationary gaps (why seldom an *inflationary* gap, I wonder?). A readings book presenting a range of views on questions of public policy is a very common adjunct to the course, but is rarely at the heart of the course.

Every few weeks, students will be given a common, objective examination, patterned after the workbook problems and exercises. These exams will be machine scored; the scores will be scaled, and each quiz section instructor will be given a suggested grade scale for his students. At the end of the term, each student will receive a grade and the mighty struggle to push back the walls of ignorance will be at an end. If Karl Marx himself were director of such a course, it would still produce more glassy-eyed boredom than red-eyed subversion.

Let me now go on to the second of my statements, to my assertion that, by and large, the economists in American colleges and universities are not all-out socialists or even unwavering critics of the market system.

Let me quote first a selection from Samuelson's textbook:

> A dramatic example of the importance of a pricing system in postwar Germany. In 1946–1947 production and consumption had dropped to a low level. Neither bombing damage nor postwar reparation payments could account for this breakdown. Paralysis of the price mechanism was clearly to blame: Money was worthless; factories closed down for lack of materials; trains could not run for lack of coal; coal could not be mined because miners were hungry; miners were hungry because peasants would not sell food for money and no industrial goods were available to give them in return. Prices were legally fixed, but little could be bought at such prices; a black market characterized by barter or fantastically high prices existed. Then in 1948 a "miracle" happened. A thorough-going currency

> reform set the price mechanism back into effective operation. Immediately production and consumption soared; again the *what, how,* and *for whom* were being resolved by markets and prices.
>
> The fact to emphasize is that such so-called miracles are going on all around us all the time—if only we look around and alert ourselves to the everyday functioning of the market.[1]

If I hadn't told you, to whom would you have ascribed those two paragraphs? Mises, Hayek, Friedman? But the paragraphs actually come from the book used by more students in America and around the world than any other book in the history of the teaching of economics.

Ah, you say, but in *other* selections Samuelson reveals his true colors. Yes, it is true; Samuelson does say much with which I disagree and with which most of you disagree. But, in common with almost all professional economists, including the best of the socialists, he does recognize the critical and necessary role of the marketplace, with an excellent, explicit development of subjective, marginalist value theory.

In a current study of mine on the impact of minimum wage laws on the Negro, I have found much good sense in the work of Samuelson and of Yale's own Lloyd Reynolds. The typical well-meaning minister or civil rights worker may urge the Negro to demand a $2.00-

---

[1] Paul Samuelson, *Economics,* 6th ed., pp. 37–38.

an-hour minimum wage—but not the typical economist.

George Stigler once wrote an article in which he argued that the study of economic theory tends to push the student in the direction of the market system, that it has a built-in-conservative bias.[2] From my own observations, I would tend to agree, much as I dislike agreeing with Stigler behind his back.

Please don't misunderstand me; I am not trying to persuade you to accept Paul Samuelson or Lloyd Reynolds or George Leland Bach or the other high priests of the introductory course into membership in the Yale Conservative Club—a suggestion that any one of the three would find decidedly amusing. Although I find much to admire and agree with in their works, I also find much with which I disagree.

But I still insist that, in spite of his faults as we would see them, the professional economist around the world (whether on this side or the other side of the iron curtain) is not our greatest enemy. Our greatest enemy is he who (whether of good intent or evil) is totally oblivious to the fact that there is a *process* at work in the economic affairs of man, that effects *are* related to causes, and that this process is a great datum of human experience. One of the brothers in Dostoevsky's classic says to the other. "There is no God and hence every-

[2] George Stigler, "The Politics of Political Economics," in *Essays in the History of Economics* (Chicago, 1965), pp. 51–65.

thing is possible." His modern counterpart says, at least by implication, "There is no Economics and hence everything is possible." Again, this is not a statement commonly made by economists, although John Kenneth Galbraith comes close to saying this in his recent writings. Perhaps Galbraith is the only economist of wisdom in America today—or perhaps (as I think more likely) Galbraith is not really an economist at all, but rather a man of letters. And men of letters, by and large, when they turn to subjects in economics, tend to produce nonsense. Thus George Bernard Shaw, self-appointed economist for the early Fabians, in his preface to *Major Barbara,* eliminates poverty everywhere with one stroke of his pen. "The thing can be done easily enough," he says, "in spite of the demonstrations to the contrary made by the economists."

Here is our real enemy, and in the struggle against him, the typical professional economist may as often be with us as against us. If he has sometimes led students into what we believe to be error, at least he has also given them basic awareness of the economic process—the beginning of economic wisdom. As always, if we who are now called "conservatives" are losing, it is because of our own weaknesses and imperfections and not because we are undone by a vicious and entrenched and invincible enemy. Let us look to our own inadequacies, not to the sins of the Paul Samuelsons, if we want to understand the mess we are in and what we can do to correct it.

Part IV

On the Business System

The two papers in this section deal with selected topics in the general area of "the business system," which occupies center stage in the drama of capitalist economics.

"Profits" was presented to a group of businessmen and clergy brought together by the National Association of Manufacturers. The meeting site was Bermuda, and the clergymen and professors in the group had an uneasy feeling that they were being "bought" by this choice of site. This uneasiness did not keep most of us from quickly signing our bar tabs against our rooms (as opposed to paying cash). It was here that I was first told by a man of the cloth that even my analysis was un-Christian.

The next paper, on the businessman, was another product of the system then prevailing at Wabash under which students were compelled to attend convocations and faculty members were "urged" to take turns as speakers. Many are the uses of adversity.

Chapter 1

Profits

"What has happened to profits?" My answer to that question is as follows: Profits have gone down. For those who think this answer inadequate, I can add the following: Profits have also been overestimated, overstated, overtaxed, underrated and misunderstood! Are there any questions?

Of course there are questions. To begin with, what proof do I have that profits have gone down? Profits after taxes in 1941 constituted 9 percent of the national income; in 1961 they constituted 5+ percent of the national income. Profits as a percentage of dollar sales averaged 5½ percent in the period 1947–49; now they are averaging 2½ to 3½. Profits as a percentage of net worth averaged 11 to 13 in the period 1947–49; now they are averaging 6 percent to 7. By any measure one can conceivably use, profits have been shrinking in the last fourteen years.

Are Profits Now Too High or Too Low?

Can we deduce from this information that profits are now too low or that they were once too high and are now just right? This is a complex question and calls for a complex and serious answer.

The first problem is to define what is meant by "too high" and "too low." Unfortunately, total dollar figures tell us almost nothing; as a matter of fact, neither do percentage figures of the kind I have given above. I am no more justified in using those figures to prove that profits are now too low than a trade union economist would be in using them to prove that profits were once too high.

The percentage share of profits in the national income of a country is largely determined by the relative abundance or scarcity of entrepreneurial capital and talent. In a country where capital is scarce and business leadership talent is in short supply, profits will and must command a larger share of the national income than in a country where both capital and talent are relatively abundant. The failure to recognize this fact is the single most important deterrent to economic growth in the underdeveloped countries of the world today. The governments of those countries, inspired in part by the antiprofits bias of both the socialists and the modern liberals, have tried to keep profit levels low, or have punished or nationalized the high-profit firms. In doing so, they have dried up the wellspring of all economic development: vigorous, aggressive entrepreneurship.

It follows as well that as an economy matures and becomes relatively better blessed with capital and leadership, the percentage share of the national income represented by profits will decline. Thus the figures I presented above do not necessarily prove that profits are now too low.

The Concept of Normal Profits

So let us abandon our inquiry into total figures. Where can we turn? One technique of explanation frequently employed is that of evaluating profit figures for the individual firm. If, for a given firm or industry, profits as a percentage return on sales or investment are found to be significantly higher than for other firms or industries, profits are said then to be "too high"; if much lower than for other firms or industries, they are said to be "too low."

This technique seems on the surface to be a valid one, and its validity is apparently attested to by the fact that even businessmen use it when they want to prove that their firms or industries are in need of help or are suffering under special handicaps.

One assumption here is that normal profits (as determined by the statistical average of all profits) are the right or "just" profits and that profits above or below normal are thus "too high" or "too low."

This approach is often used by trade unions to show that a given group of firms has been making abnormally large profits and thus can and should pay higher wages.

It is extremely unfortunate that this point of view on profits has received such wide acceptance in all groups in our society. It implies that businesses should be permitted (perhaps even assisted) to make a "normal" or "fair" profit, but become suspect once they earn more than this statistical norm.

This approach rests on a serious misunderstanding of the function of profits and losses in a free market economy. It is true that, in the long run, and in a competitive market, each firm will be making profits no more and no less than it could make in alternative activities. This is true because if the typical firm in the industry were making higher than normal profits, other firms would enter the industry and profits would be driven down. If the typical firm were making lower than normal profits, some firms would leave the industry and profits for those remaining would rise. Thus in the long run profits *do* tend to be at the so-called normal or average level.

However, at a given moment of time in a changing, dynamic economy, few firms or industries will be in this long-run equilibrium position. Most will be in the process of making adjustments to the changing circumstances. Thus, in some industries, profits will be well above normal, and in others, profits will be well below normal.

It is this fact which leads the firms involved to make the adjustments called for in the service of consumers. The abnormally high profits in some industries are the signal that consumers are calling for more firms to enter those industries. The below-normal profits or outright losses in other industries are the signal that consumers are calling for some firms to get out.

The importance of this signal system can be illustrated by the life history of the ball-point pen. When Reynolds produced the first ball-point pen, he sold it for around $12.95. It is doubtful if, even then, production and distribution costs were as much as one fourth of the selling price. By any measure known to man, Reynolds was receiving abnormally high profits. However, the signal went out loud and clear; soon every pen company had its ball-point pens, and new firms entered the field almost daily. Within a short period of time, the price of the pens had dropped below $5.00. Now I am writing this paper with a pen that I bought with nine others for a total cost of $1.19 for the ten.

Suppose the government, shocked by Reynolds' profits, had insisted on recapturing all of his profits above a return of (say) 6 percent on capital and made this a universal rule for the industry. Or suppose that Reynolds' workers had insisted on their wages being increased until his profits were brought down to "normal." In either case, the price of ball-point pens might well still be $12.95. But because the abnormally high profits were permitted to serve as a signal to other producers, the results were as I have described them above.

The above-normal profits then are not "too high" in any value sense, nor are the below-normal profits "too low." They are simply signals and very, very important signals as well. In fact, the efficiency of the economy is completely dependent upon their not being silenced or modified.

Nor is this signal system costly to the consumer it serves. Abnormally high profits in some areas tend to be balanced by below-normal profits in other areas, and the net cost to the consumer is minimal.

If the consumer insists on recapturing the excess profits, surely he is compelled by logic and conscience to indemnify those who are getting below-normal profits, and the net gain would be of no immediate significance. The price of doing so, though, would be the destruction of the combined signal and incentive system of the free market—and hence his hope for a free and prosperous society.

In the same way, the worker who would demand that wages be tied to profits, that the employer share the excess profits with him, should be compelled by logic and conscience then to take wage cuts whenever his firm is making below-average profits. Few workers would have much enthusiasm for the arrangement thus presented.

In sum, then, we gain little insight into what has happened to profits by asking if some firms are making profits above or below the average. Such deviations from the average are a normal and indispensable part of the functioning of the competitive market economy.

The Concept of Market Structure

We seem now to have thrown out all meaningful ways of evaluating profits, of determining what has happened to profits. Perhaps we should give up in despair and turn our attention to some other problem.

Fortunately, there still remain certain indirect approaches to the problem that do have meaning. Let me go back to a phrase I have used several times, "the competitive market." *It is literally true that profits never can be said to be too high or too low in a competitive market.* In such a market, forces are always at work to bring profits back to the normal level, and the net cost to the consumer is minimal.

But what if the markets in which the firms deal are not competitive? What then of profits?

If a given firm has a monopoly of its market, it may be said to make above-normal profits and to make them indefinitely. The signal is going out, but the other firms are prevented by the monopoly power of this one firm from answering the signal. Under these circumstances it is quite meaningful and realistic to say that profits are "too high."

Again, if the firm is selling in a competitive market, but buying its resources (for example, its labor services) from units that are not competing, it may suffer from a cost squeeze on profits that will cause those profits to be persistently below normal. In the short run, the owners of the firm will suffer, and, in the long run, the consumer will suffer as firms will get out of the industry in response to a basically false or distorted below-normal profit signal. Here again it is quite meaningful and realistic to say that profits are "too low."

Our search then must take us to the markets of this country, to ask whether product and resource markets are less or more competitive than they once were or than they could or should be.

Product Markets

Let us begin with the selling side, with product markets. It is commonly assumed that the American business firm was once small in size and competitive, but that it is now large in size and monopolistic.

This is a complex subject which cannot be explored fully in limited space. However, here are my views in brief form.

(1) I believe that it can be demonstrated that product markets in America are more competitive today than they have ever been. My reasoning is that, though firms have grown in size, markets have grown even more rapidly. The absolute size of the actual firm is unimportant. What is important is its size *relative* to the industry or market in which it operates.

Improvements in transportation and communication and the development of substitutes for almost any and every kind of product have so widened markets that neither A&P nor U.S. Steel has as much real market power as did the small town grocery store and the local iron foundry a century ago!

(2) I believe that such instances of monopoly as do arise tend to be rather quickly erased by the dynamic changes in the economy.

(3) I believe that almost all instances of *persistent* monopoly power that do exist can be attributed to positive protection of that power by government. The protection take such forms as price supports in agriculture, tariffs, fair trade laws, special franchises and licenses, subsidies, etc.

(4) I believe that the unhampered market naturally tends to be a competitive market. Monopoly is not only unnatural, but can be maintained only with the positive support of government.

If what I have written above is true, then we can add that profits are not generally "too high" in the American economy, except in those cases where the government is giving direct or indirect support to monopoly power. NOTE: Profits can be "too high" even if they are in fact losses! Thus if the government is subsidizing or otherwise aiding a declining industry, losses will be less than in a free market. Thus, returns to the firms involved are "too high" in that they do not accurately reflect the true signal being sent out by consumers. Excess resources will be held in the industry long after the consumer has ordered them out! A case in point would be agriculture.

Resource Markets

We turn now to the buying side of the markets in which firms operate: to the resource markets. Are these markets less or more competitive than they used to be, or than they can or should be?

This too is a complex question and again I can do no more than summarize my argument.

(1) I believe that the resource markets also tend to be competitive in the absence of government intervention. Improved transportation and communication have expanded alternatives confronting both the buyer and the seller of most resources, including labor.

(2) However, governments have been particularly active in labor markets in the last thirty years and have done much to force the employer to hire his labor in noncompetitive markets. Governments have done this through direct setting of wages, hours, and working conditions and by encouraging, protecting, and giving special privileges to trade unions.

(3) I believe that the effect of this has been to make of the trade union a government-sponsored instrument for distorting the workings of the market. It has resulted in a never-ending cost squeeze on profits in large segments of the American economy.

If what I have said above is true, then it follows that what has happened to profits is that they tend to be "too low" in those segments of the American economy most influenced by trade unionism and by wage legislation. NOTE: Profits can be "too low" even though the firm is making above-normal profits! Thus, in an expanding industry, wage increases can hold profits below the levels they would otherwise have reached. Thus the high-profit signal is somewhat muffled and resources may not be entering the industry at the rate consumers are ordering them to!

The Impact of Taxes

This tendency is reinforced by the taxing process. Both the fact and the form of profits taxes tend to reduce the effectiveness of the signal system. The effect is one-sided in that profitable industries have their returns taxed by the government, but unprofitable industries do not receive subsidies—nor should they. Permission to do some spreading of losses does not help firms in industries that are expanding and generally profitable, year after year. Moreover, the unrealistic handling of depreciation in an environment of inflation leads to persistent overstating and hence overtaxing of business earnings.

Summary

I have argued that most of the usual ways of evaluating profits are meaningless. I have suggested that profits can best be examined *indirectly,* by weighing them in the context of the markets in which firms buy and sell. I have expressed my belief that the greatest distortion in those markets in America today is in the labor areas, and that, as a consequence of this distortion and of other factors, profits tend to be "too low" in large segments of American industry.

I would add that this fact goes a long way to explain the persistence of unemployment in an apparently prosperous nation. The general business climate created by government interventions, particularly in the labor markets, is not one that creates buoyancy and optimism in the business world. Thus, the economy tends to sag, and adjustments are not quickly made. More directly, unemployment tends to be concentrated in those industries and those areas most influenced by aggressive union action in the last thirty years.

If these "low low" profits persist, the economy is in danger of being moved even further from the free-market ideal. The apparent failure or refusal of private enterprise to "do the job" will lead Americans to demand more and more government intervention (witness the demand for deficit spending to "get the country going").

The solution lies not in raising profits by granting special favors to business (as is so often suggested) but rather in reducing or eliminating the special handicaps business has faced in its labor markets and in other ways during recent decades.

If this is not done, we are in danger of losing our free economy; and when economic freedom is lost, all other freedoms must follow, sooner or later.

Chapter 2

The Businessman

I should like to begin with a paragraph from an article in a recent issue of the *Wall Street Journal.* The headlines read as follows: "Scorning business. More college students shun corporate jobs, choose other fields. Teaching, Peace Corps lure Harvard grads: company hiring quotas go unfilled. Martinis, ulcers and profits."

In the article proper, Roger Ricklefs writes:

> The word on the campus is that business is for the birds. At college after college an increasing percentage of graduates is shunning business careers in favor of such fields as teaching, scientific research, law and public service. Amherst College says that 48 percent of its alumni are businessmen, but fewer than 20 percent of recent graduates have been entering business. Only 14 percent of last spring's Harvard graduates plan business careers, down from 39 percent five years ago. Arthur Lyon Dahl, a June graduate of Stanford University, says of his classmates:

> "I know of almost no one who even considered a business career."
>
> One of the toughest obstacles confronting company recruiters on many campuses is a general atmosphere of scorn for business.

This last sentence has suggested my question for this morning. Can any right-thinking young man deliberately choose a career in the business world?

Is being a businessman a respectable way to go through life? You will note, I am not asking if any *particular* person should be a businessman. There are many for whom other careers are clearly indicated. I am asking only if it is one of the acceptable alternatives confronting a young person today.

I raise this question because I have a feeling that, on most college campuses today, a student could easily gain the impression that if he chooses a career in business, he will have embarrassed the college, his teachers and his yet unborn children.

I wish now to examine some of the more common campus views of the businessman to see to what extent they are valid descriptions of life in the gray flannel suit.

The first is the view that whatever else it is, a career in business is not a life spent in serving the human race, in doing something for others. If this were accepted by all, there would of course be no businessmen in this world, because it is almost literally impossible for the average man to spend his life doing something which he thinks is of no value to others. Even the drug pusher or the prostitute is led to insist that his or her role is an extremely important one in serving the emotional needs of society.

I take as granted then your desire to do something useful to serve society. Can you do it as a businessman? That many still answer "no" to this question is a tribute to the enduring quality of an old myth—the myth that in an exchange, what one party gains, the other must lose. In a voluntary exchange, both parties must expect to gain or no exchange will take place. A businessman is a specialist in voluntary exchange, and his success is largely determined by how well he succeeds in serving others.

Don't I really mean, by how well he succeeds in *deceiving* others into *thinking* he is serving them? Isn't a kind of sophisticated dishonesty a requirement for success in business? I make no claims for the superior moral fiber of the businessman, but I will say this: A basically dishonest man can survive longer in the church or the classroom than he can in the grain exchange or the furniture business. The penalty system in the business world operates with some real precision and certainty, largely unencumbered by a mystique of occupational sanctification.

There *are* dishonest men in the business world, of course, but if you go into the business world, you will be under no greater pressure to stretch the truth than if you get a job as an editor of a college catalogue or as a speechwriter for candidates for political office or a member of Nader's Raiders.

But doesn't the businessman, if he wants to get ahead, have to cater to the whims and caprices of his customers, no matter how depraved their tastes might be? Yes, of course; that is, he must serve other people as those other people wish to be served and not as he thinks they *ought* to want to be served. This may be what rules out the businessman as a public servant. The public servant is perhaps a man who serves others as they *ought* to be served, rather than as they *want* to be served or perhaps more accurately, as they are willing to pay to be served.

Now don't misunderstand me; I have great respect for the man who says, "This is what I think it right to paint, or compose, or produce; if you like it, fine. If you don't, fine. If you want to pay me for it, fine; if you don't, fine." This is a position of integrity and honesty; it is also a position rarely encountered in the business world. But let's be honest with each other. It is not really the position of one who serves others, but rather of one who serves some personal set of imperatives. Moreover, it may enable you to make a living or it may not. If you have the guts for this kind of stance, go to it. Just don't complain later that no one recognizes your talent with monthly paychecks.

If you *are* interested in making a living, then you are usually well advised to take some account of what others are willing to pay to get. Admittedly there is a way out; rather than serving B as B is willing to pay to be served, A can sometimes be paid with C's money to do for B for free what he, A, knows to be best for B. This, by the way, is more in keeping with the modern concept of public service than is the direct exchange with B on a quid pro quo basis.

Whatever the case, you *can,* in fact, *must* serve others if you wish to be a businessman. I would go so far as to argue that the young man who goes to a country like Brazil as an employee of (say) Sears Roebuck will end up doing more real good for the people of the country than will the young man who goes there as a member of the Peace Corps. This is not an argument against the Peace Corps, which is largely meant to be symbolic anyway. But it is an argument for giving some thought to Sears Roebuck, even though you would be paid more by Sears than the Peace Corps.

Now that we've mentioned the embarrassing topic of compensation, perhaps we should pursue it for a moment. Isn't the businessman, by definition, a person who is primarily concerned with making the almighty dollar?

Well, motives differ, even among businessmen, but I am not going to deny that most businessmen are trying to make money. This may or may not be an admirable objective in life. I would say this: the serving of this idol probably produces, not only less of heroism and glory, but also less of cruelty, fanaticism, and bloodshed than does the serving of such idols as patriotism or the one true church or the New Jerusalem. As I remember it, neither Socrates nor Christ nor Servetus nor Joan of Arc was put to death by a frustrated business rival. As Samuel Johnson put it, "A man is never more innocently involved than in the making of money."

But even in this the businessman differs from the typical nonbusinessman only in degree. Most lawyers and doctors I have known have been able to restrain their impulses to offer their services free to one and all.

What of the college teacher? I can honestly say that I know of almost no men or women who have entered college teaching with a view to getting rich. Yet, once in the profession, we have been known to bargain for the limited prizes available in our profession with an aggressiveness that would bring a blush to the cheeks of the operator of an oriental bazaar.

A life that measures itself in terms of income alone is not likely to be a noble one, but there is no requirement that all who enter the business world must display more than a normal, prudent regard for their own and their family's financial well-being.

Now to another question: Even if all that I've said is true, isn't it also true that the business world offers no real intellectual challenges and that the businessman becomes, over time, a culturally deprived person?

Those who argue that there are no intellectual challenges in the business world simply do not know of what they are speaking. Nor are the challenges limited to those working in the pure research section of R & D. Conrad, in *Lord Jim,* says of the man who serves as water-clerk for a supply firm that "he must have ability in the Abstract and demonstrate it practically." This is true of all roles of any significance in the business world, and the intellectual challenge in such roles is hard and clear. These roles call for imagination and for analytical skills of no mean order.

Now it is perfectly true that the business world rarely calls for intellectuality of the bookish variety. If you want to spend your full working day dealing with ideas, both your own and others, then the business world is not for you. You should join those of us who are professional intellectuals.

All that I am saying is that the business world requires the use of the intellect; it is not a kind of lotus land for the mind. Nor do you need lose *all* interest in the *bookish* variety of intellectuality. Wallace Stevens combined his career as an insurance executive with his other role as a poet. Crawford Greenewalt, once Chairman of the Board of the Du Pont Company, has written a definitive work on the hummingbird. The men who buy the works of art, who attend the concerts, who fill the theaters are in the main drudges from the world of business—and this in spite of the fact that in the usual Broadway play, the businessman is portrayed as either a knave or a fool. Many businessmen have no intellectual interests of this kind, but it *is* possible to be a businessman without also being a Philistine.

One final objection: Do not the pressures for conformity in the business world effectively silence whatever human or intellectual impulses a man may have taken with him into that world? I am referring here of course to the concept of the organizational man. I can't deny that the business organization does exert both formal and informal pressures on the individual to conform to certain patterns, although I think the extent of conformity demanded has been seriously exaggerated. But the most important point is this: *Any* organization you join, whether business, educational, governmental, or philanthropic, subjects you to this problem. The organization man is found wherever organization is found. If you really want to be subjected to *no* pressures of this kind, then you'd better decide here and now to go it on your own, whatever you do—whether it's teaching history or producing glassware.

Let me illustrate: I would wager that there was more informal pressure on the typical college faculty member during the election of 1964 to conform to the prevailing campus anti-Goldwaterism than there was pressure on any businessman to conform to the prevailing conservatism of his class. Or to put it another way: Some of the most slavish conformists I know are those who are conforming to some in-group type of nonconformity.

If you wish to work with other people, your integrity is measured not by whether you recognize their needs and interests, not by whether you accept compromise solutions, but by your choice of those things where compromise is possible and necessary and of those things where you must never compromise. If you can't accept even this, then find yourself a Walden Pond and go with my blessing.

So much for my case for the poor, misunderstood businessman. I am not arguing that the businessman is a hero or a saint, or that all businessmen are great guys who compose sonnets in Italian on the side, or that all of you should run from here to the placement office to sign up for the next interview. I am saying only that in deciding on a career, as in everything else, you should decide on the basis of reasonably accurate information. I suppose I could summarize it this way: The problem on the typical college campus is not that so many people know so little about the businessman; the problem is that so many know so much about the businessman that isn't so.

Part V

On Labor Markets

This paper was presented as a meeting of the Midwest Economics Association in 1957. It was later printed in *Business Topics,* a journal published by the School of Business at Michigan State University. As you will see, its message was not such as to bring me invitations to speak at trade union conventions—or at meetings of those pushing for right-to work laws either.

Chapter 1

The Labor Monopoly

In the paragraphs to follow you will find me critical of both the goals and techniques of trade unionism. Nor can I soften this position by announcing that, in spite of my sharp words, I am basically pro-union. I am not for "good" but opposed to "bad" (e.g., racket-controlled) trade unionism. I am not for "responsible," but opposed to "irresponsible" trade unionism. I am simply not pro-union, period. I can no more be pro-union than I can be pro- the Southern California Fruit Growers' Association or pro- the Retail Druggists Association of America.

But there is worse to come: I am not even anti-union but pro-labor. I cannot direct my concern to one man rather than another simply because one is a laborer and the other an entrepreneur or a landowner or even (God help us!) a member of the *rentier* class.

But, as W. C. Fields once said, "No man who hates both dogs and children can be altogether bad," and I will confess to one weakness. I am persuaded that proper economic policy requires that we fix our gaze steadily on the long-run interests of the consumer and ignore all else. Surely you are prepared by now for a quotation from Adam Smith, and here it is:

> Consumption is the sole end and purpose of all production; and the interest of the producer ought to be attended to only so far as it may be necessary for promoting that of the consumer. The maxim is so perfectly self-evident, that it would be absurd to attempt to prove it.[1]

As a matter of fact, in the modern literature on my specific topic, the labor monopoly, I have found almost nothing that was not explicitly and intelligently discussed in *The Wealth of Nations*. My regret is that our public policy in this area has moved so far from his wise counsel.

In effect, Adam Smith proposed that unions be tolerated but in no way encouraged or granted special privileges and immunities. This was Adam Smith's position and it is also mine. In the sections to follow I shall present the reasoning and the value judgments that lead me to take this position.

I
Review of Opposing Views

I am aware that the policy position I have taken is not consistent with the present policy of this country.

[1] Adam Smith, *The Wealth of Nations* (New York: Modern Library, 1937), p. 625.

I am keenly aware of the fact that it is not only opposed by but is deeply disturbing to many persons, both in and out of the academic world, whose good will and intelligence I respect. Both this respect and the desire to make my reasoning, my assumptions, and my judgments as explicit as possible impel me to state why I cannot accept the conventional policy of the government or the conventional wisdom that supports it.

In beginning this review of the various shadings of the conventional wisdom, I must apologize for the obvious oversimplification and distortion of individual positions that is involved in creating such useful and meaningful but arbitrary groupings as "the human-relations group" and "the labor economist group."

The Human-Relations Approach

Perhaps the most extreme position is that taken by the personnel, human-relations group. To the members of this group, the question of whether there is or is not a labor monopoly is simply irrelevant. It is irrelevant because monopoly is a market-type word and they have decided that the market doesn't exist. Recently I scanned a collection of books with titles such as "Human Relations in Industry" and was dismayed to find that my discipline, economics, is obsolete.

Thus Norman Maier in his book, *Psychology in Industry,* writes, "Except in very general ways the law of supply and demand no longer applies to labor."[2] Joseph

[2] Norman Maier, *Psychology in Industry* (New York: Houghton Mifflin, 1955), p. 6.

Tiffin in the book, *Industrial Psychology,* writes, "In general, management as well as labor is becoming less and less dependent on the so-called 'law' of supply and demand as a basic factor in determining wage rates."[3]

And so it goes. As Kenneth Boulding of the University of Michigan once said in a discussion of this topic, everywhere he turns he finds labor economists and industrial relations specialists jumping up and down on the corpse of supply and demand and proclaiming, "the labor market is dead; long live human relations."

Of course it is patently true that neither the employer nor the worker looks with favor on the labor market process as it impinges disadvantageously on him. To paraphrase St. Augustine, each is saying, "Oh Lord, make me be forced to compete, but not yet." The human relations experts say, "not yet, or ever." Many of them look with horror on the competitive struggle of the marketplace and on the conflict of the employer and employee over division of the product. They seem to imagine that the "right" system of industrial relations can be developed which will generate in each firm such a feeling of togetherness that, hand in hand, employer and employee will march joyously into the New Jerusalem.

Attractive as this picture is, I am nonetheless con-

---

[3] Joseph Tiffin, *Industrial Psychology* (New York: Prentice-Hall, 1952), p. 362.

vinced that neither employer nor employee nor human-relations expert will like what he will get if we continue to move away from the labor market, if we insist that the services of labor must not be subjected to the vulgar calculus of the marketplace.

If the employer does succeed in insulating his own workers from the temptations of the marketplace, he will find that he must then take care of them through thick or thin and that the guaranteed annual wage will have to give way to the guaranteed lifetime wage. He will also find that his motivation problems have assumed staggering proportions. Good human relations or lousy human relations, the worker you can neither fire nor promote on the basis of performance is going to be a hard worker to stir into action.

But the worker too will find his security a very mixed blessing. To discover too late that he has made an unwise first decision and yet to be condemned by the weight of seniority and other considerations to that job is likely to be a frustrating experience. The old freedom to pick and move will be gone, because of course to move would be to threaten another man's job and hence his property. Even the union that administers this job security system will find it a mixed blessing. The workers will now turn their ambitions to control of the controllers and the fights for power within the unions will be bitter and bloody. Moreover, the amount of power exercised by the leadership over the economic process will be so tempting that cases of corruption and racketeering will be commonplace. These circumstances may in turn engender such a great amount of public ill will that the unions will find themselves more and more under the control and guidance of government. Even the human-relations expert will be disappointed to find that competition and conflict can go on outside the marketplace. In fact the nonmarket conflict is likely to be more personal and hence more degrading than the old market-channeled conflict.

In sum, neither the employer nor the employee nor the human-relations expert is likely to approve of what he will get, if he gets what he now seems to want. The question of the impact of the trade union on a market economy cannot be assumed away by assuming away the labor market.

The Macroeconomic Approach

I turn now to the economists and find in many of them a like tendency to consider the labor monopoly issue, at least in its typical concerns, to be largely irrelevant. For example, to one group of economists, the microeconomic or individual-market aspects of labor monopoly are of little interest. What is important is the impact of wage determinations on the income- and employment-determining aggregates. Thus trade union influence on wage rates is of significance primarily as it affects beneficially or adversely the chances of the economy's attaining and maintaining full employment.

Thus, if unions have increased the downward rigidity of wage rates, they may have introduced a valuable expectations-damping factor in deflationary movements. Similarly, the redistributive effects of wage increases may move the average propensity to consume in the right direction at the right time.

I have no doubt but that trade-union action may coincidentally and occasionally serve the interests of economic stability; but I also have no doubt that it may coincidentally and occasionally work directly contrary to the purposes of economic stability, particularly in an inflationary environment. For the effect to be always the right one would require a degree of social control of trade-union policy that is not likely to be asked or granted in our society. Surely the interests of economic stability can be served by techniques more certain in effect and with fewer unwanted side effects than trade unionism.

The Approach of the Labor Economists

Leaving the macroeconomic approach, I now turn to the approach of the labor economists. It is always dangerous to ascribe a point of view to a group in which there may be a considerable range of opinion, but still I find a surprising homogeneity of approach in the textbooks on labor economics.

In general the authors of these books treat the central question of labor monopoly with rare delicacy and with esthetically remarkable displays of verbal footwork. In many of the books, the word *monopoly* is not even in the index. Note the care with which the author of the following passage has handled this question.

> To return to the original question as to whether unions are monopolies, there is no doubt they hold some degree of monopoly power. That is their nature and purpose, and we give them legal protection with the specific aim of increasing the bargaining (i.e., monopoly) power of labor. In only rare instances do unions actually control the supply of labor to a firm or occupation, and their freedom to do so should not (in the opinion of the author) be protected. But to say that unions hold monopoly power leaves the important questions unanswered. When and where is the monopoly power of the union clearly stronger than the monopsony power of the employer, and what are the best techniques for removing the discrepancy—or the reverse discrepancy? How can we prevent undue injury to the public from disagreements between union and management in essential industries? These and many other unanswered questions illustrate the pointlessness of discussing the problem of unions in the framework of monopoly analysis, and point to the direction in which the answers—if, indeed, there are any—are to be found.[4]

J. M. Clark has phrased it as follows: "We are opposed to monopoly; when we find a kind we do not want to oppose, we will call it by a different name."[5]

---

[4] Alfred Kuhn, *Labor Institutions and Economics* (New York: Rinehart & Co., 1956), pp. 594–95.

[5] J. M. Clark in *The Impact of the Union,* ed. David McCord Wright (New York: Kelley and Millman, 1956), p. 364.

It may be true that a trade union does not match the description of classical enterprise monopoly in every detail. But its goal of manipulating the market to extract an advantage for those involved is certainly a monopoly-type goal. Personally, if I were paying dues to a union, I would most certainly feel cheated if the union leaders refused to act like monopolists, if they made no attempt to manipulate the market in my favor. I may question whether trade unions in America have in fact been able to exercise strong monopoly power, but I can never question their desire to do so.

Having denied that unions try to or do exercise monopoly power, the labor economists go on to state that unions use their monopoly power to combat the monopsony power of the employers. Here at last is the classical case for trade unionism.

The relevant question would seem to be the following: Do employers in fact possess monopsony power in the labor markets in which they operate? Certainly they would like to do so and often attempt to do so. But I see nothing in the history of wage rates in this country and in comparisons of union and non-union industry experience that would lead me to conclude that employers in this country do now or have ever exercised significant monopsony power in the labor markets. The weakness of the individual worker in obtaining "fair" wages is one of the most durable and widely believed myths in the economic folklore of the modern world.

Even my hero, Adam Smith, gave it some standing, though it may have possessed some greater validity in his day than in ours. Today's worker, with his far greater physical and psychological mobility, need hardly sit still to be exploited, and a solid core of movable workers will protect even those who have little or no mobility, just as I am protected in buying television sets by those who are shrewd enough to know that it is not magic but easily understood processes which cause them to work.

It is my firm belief that, as a general rule, workers need trade unions, not to assure themselves of roughly competitive wages, but only to assure themselves of wages *above* what the competitive market would assign them. If this fits in with our value system, let us endorse it, but let us at least be honest about it.

Now whether, through trade unionism, workers can *in fact* gain wages significantly different from what a competitive market would produce for them is itself a debatable question. I am inclined to agree with Milton Friedman, of the University of Chicago, and others who argue that the economic impact of unions has been exaggerated by both their friends and their foes. Admittedly, they have been more successful in some industries than in others, and the joint-demand approach gives us a pretty good explanation of why this should be. Also, they have been most successful when they have been able to enlist the direct or indirect support of government in their activities. Thus, my barber informs me that a non-union barbershop in Indiana is almost certain to be found unsanitary by the state inspection teams, while a union barbershop can get by with almost anything. (This, by the way, is what passes for research among college deans.)

In minimizing the influence of unions on wage levels and structures, I do not mean to say that unions cause no problems. Certainly, union action is capable of inconveniencing large segments of the American economy. Certainly, unions can and do interfere with the efficient use of workers and machines in the individual plants and thus tend to lower the overall productivity of the economy. And certainly, they constitute at least a latent political pressure group of great strength and, from my point of view, of dangerous and mistaken social philosophy. Yet, paradoxically, I am disturbed by our interfering with the right of union members to spend union funds in support of parties and candidates.

These and other problems do arise; however, I do not believe that unions have in fact been able to produce any generally significant changes in the level or structure of wages in this country.

But whether unions do or do not succeed in accomplishing what they wish to accomplish is not the important question. The important question is what should be the policy of the country toward a group that *seeks* to manipulate the market to the advantage of its members.

II
Criticism of Current Policy

The American answer of this century has been that government should encourage and protect this particular group, the trade unionists, as they seek to organize and to manipulate the market. This answer seems to have been based in part on the countervailing power thesis, in part on certain ideas of distributive justice, in part on the great American tradition of siding with the underdog.

Whatever the reasons were that led to this position being adopted, it has resulted in a series of legislative enactments, starting with the Clayton Act and various railway acts, which have given unions special privileges and immunities enjoyed by no other group in our economy.[6] Surely this approach directly violates one of the traditional philosophical positions of our society, namely, equality before the law.

The special privileges of trade unions have been imaginatively described by Edward Chamberlin of Harvard University, in the following passage:

> If A is bargaining with B over the sale of his house, and if A were given the privileges of a modern labor union, he

[6] See listings in Roscoe Pound, *Legal Immunities of Labor Unions* (Washington, D.C.: American Enterprise Association, 1957); Sylvester Petro, *The Labor Policy of the Free Society* (New York: Ronald Press, 1957).

> would be able (1) to conspire with all other owners of houses not to make any alternative offer to B, using violence or the threat of violence if necessary to prevent them, (2) to deprive B himself of access to any alternative offers, (3) to surround the house of B and cut off all deliveries, including food (except by parcel post), (4) to stop all movement from B's house, so that if he were for instance a doctor he could not sell his services and make a living, and (5) to institute a boycott of B's business. All of these privileges, if he were capable of carrying them out, would no doubt strengthen A's position. But they would not be regarded by anyone as part of "bargaining"—unless A were a labor union.[7]

Surely if we must favor income redistribution (which I do not), we can find ways of implementing our wishes that do not violate the concepts of rule of law and equality before the law.

III
Conclusions

What then am I proposing? I am proposing that we place trade unionism on the same basis as all other groupings in our economy and that whatever rules apply to the others would apply to unions as well. I am not proposing that we legislate unions out of existence. I am proposing only that we treat them as we should

[7] Edward H. Chamberlin, *The Economic Analysis of Labor Union Power* (Washington, D.C.: American Enterprise Association, 1958), pp. 41–42.

treat all collections of people seeking to manipulate the market. For the proper policy I turn again to Adam Smith and to the famous passage in which he outlines his approach to collusion among businessmen:

> People of the same trade seldom meet together, even for merriment and diversion, but the conversation ends in a conspiracy against the public, or in some contrivance to raise prices. It is impossible indeed to prevent such meetings, by any law which either could be executed, or would be consistent with liberty and justice. But though the law cannot hinder people of the same trade from sometimes assembling together, it ought to do nothing to facilitate such assemblies; much less to render them necessary.[8]

This was his approach to trade unionism as well, and this approach was substantially the one that developed under American common law and was controlling until the legislative enactments of this century. Unions were tolerated, but not encouraged, and were granted no special privileges, no immunities from the law of the land. I would suggest that we return the problems of trade unionism to the jurisdiction of the common law, which would mean sweeping away the relevant sections of the Clayton Act and the railway acts, as well as all of the Norris-LaGuardia Act, the Wagner Act, and the Taft-Hartley Act.

I realize that at this moment many of you do not

---

[8] Adam Smith, *The Wealth of Nations* (New York: Modern Library, 1937), p. 128.

know whether to laugh or cry. But let me sketch for you what seems to me to be the most likely path of movement in the years ahead. The relative popularity of state right-to-work laws is an important straw in the wind. It symbolizes the kind of authoritarian answer to unions that is almost certain to become more popular in the years ahead.

To me the right-to-work law is an unwarranted intrusion by the state in the dealings of employers and employees. If an employer and his workers agree that only Presbyterians or Masons or union members will be employed in the plant, the state has no business interfering in that agreement. (I might add that the state also has no right interfering in agreements that would limit employment to non-union workers; i.e., in outlawing yellow-dog contracts.)

As a matter of fact, in proposing right-to-work laws the political conservative is weakening his case against trade unionism. In developing his case for right-to-work laws, he argues that workers *cannot* escape the exploiting union; but in developing his case against trade unions, he argues that workers *can* escape the would-be exploiting employer. My own guess is that the exceptions to the sufficient-mobility requirement are about as numerous and significant in one case as in the other—and that in neither are the exceptions of sufficient impact or duration to justify special legislation.

If you believe that the state should not intervene in

dealings between employers and employees, then that means not only no Wagner Acts, but no right-to-work laws and no administrative review of wage settlements as well. Yet we seem to be headed for ever more intervention by the state in dealings between employers and employees, in the internal affairs of unions and in the wage-price relationships in industry. Having created our Frankenstein monster, we are now going to break him to our will.

In the process the state is almost certain to undertake to dictate decisions about matters that should be left to the marketplace, and to create authoritarian patterns of action that will be degrading and debilitating to employers and employees alike. Unions were able to survive the times of adversity; whether they will be able to survive their successes is open to question.

If this forecast of the shape of things to come be even partly correct, then a suggestion that we review the legislative enactments of the last fifty years is not as ridiculous as it might seem at first blush. Failing a basic change in philosophy of the kind I have outlined, I see nothing but increasing difficulty in the years ahead. I have made my proposal in absolute seriousness and with no desire simply to shock or antagonize.

I am aware that it is difficult to "turn back the clock," but if we were convinced that it should be done, I suspect that we could find ways of doing it. I am also under no illusions that a full acceptance of my proposal would mean the end of all the vexing problems that arise in the employment relationship. Starting as I do with the assumption that man is imperfect, I can hardly arrive at the conclusion that he can create a utopia. The choices must always be among various degrees of imperfection, and the choice I have made seems to be the least imperfect of those now available.

Part VI

On Money and Inflation

In this section, I deal with that most ubiquitous of all diseases of economic life: inflation. As Lenin predicted, it is fast becoming the instrument of the disintegrating process in capitalist economies—though its ravages are equally visible in the socialist economies of the world.

The first paper is one version of a long-run-economic-outlook speech that I have been giving to various groups for a number of years. Given the bleakness of the outlook presented here, I wish that I could report that events have given the lie to my prophecies, but such does not seem to be the case.

The second paper, "Alleged Causes of Inflation: Corporate Monopolies," was presented in March 1976 at the fourth annual conference of the Committee for Monetary Research and Education, held at Arden House, Harriman, New York.

Chapter 1

The Long-Run Economic Outlook

The most probable course of events in the American economy in the next ten to fifteen years is the following: (1) continuing, in fact, accelerating inflation; (2) no major depression, but occasional periods of reduced real output (and hence employment); (3) off-and-on price and wage controls; (4) a rising pattern of interest rates; (5) an increasing direction of private economic activity by public agencies; and (6) an increasingly hampered economy, with an associated decline in its efficiency and its capacity to produce economic growth. The most probable final outcome of all this is that the American economy will come to look very much like the English economy of today, an economy that one English observer has described as "sinking slowly under the sea, giggling as she goes down."

The reasons for this probable course of events are many and complex. However, many of those reasons relate to what I believe to be serious misconceptions about what inflation is, what causes it, and what it can and cannot produce.

Misconceptions about Inflation

(1) The primordial sin in treating of inflation is that of assuming that interest rates can be kept at some desired level (usually "low") by increasing the money supply, i.e., by an easy money policy. It is typically argued that high interest rates reduce investment, curtail output, reduce home building, penalize the debtor-poor to the advantage of the creditor-rich, etc., and that low interest rates are clearly to be preferred to high. This argument is filled with dubious connections, but the *real* trouble flows from the attempt to implement its thesis by means of continuous inflation.

The fact of the matter is that the level of interest rates is a market phenomenon, and not only is it undesirable for government to seek to control it but it is largely impossible for it to do so as well. It is true that by adding to or subtracting from the rate of change in the money stock, *temporary* changes, particularly in short-term rates, can be achieved—and this illusion of effectiveness is the precise source of the problem. Suppose for example that the monetary authority (i.e., the Federal Reserve System) were to bring about a significant injection of new money into the economic stream over a short period of time. The point of impact of the injection would normally be the short-term money market, and the rather immediate consequence would be a fall in the short-term rate of interest. However, over the course of the next few months, as this new money churned through the economy, there would be a tendency for spending of all kinds to increase, with consequent upward pressure on prices. This in turn would lead both businesses and individuals to wish to spend more now, to build up inventories or undertake expansion of plant, or buy durables and homes *now* before prices go even higher. This increased propensity to spend would be translated into a sharply increased demand for loanable funds. This in turn would mean that the original increase in the quantity of money would be offset by the increased demand for loanable funds, and interest rates would start to climb. Moreover, as potential lenders would see prices rising, they would insist on an inflation premium in the interest rate; in other words, the supply curve of loanable funds would shift up and to the left, indicating that it would now take a higher rate to bring forth a given volume of loanable funds than was true before.

But why can't this countering effect be matched or more than matched by continuing injections of new money? Because this would mean continuing inflation and this in turn would mean a demand by lenders for an even higher inflation premium on interest rates.

To try to cure the problem of high interest rates by increasing the quantity of money, i.e., by inflation, is like trying to cure a hangover by some "hair of the dog" the next morning. The temporary feeling of well-being is closely followed by a renewed attack of the problem; the alleged remedy is in fact not a cure to the problem but its precise cause. It is inflation that causes high interest rates, not the reverse, the Honorable Wright Patman to the contrary. There is one way and only one way to bring the market rate of interest back to the levels we tend to think of as normal, and that is to take the inflation premium out of interest rates by taking the inflation out of the economy—and there is only one way to do that, and that is by keeping the quantity of money from going up faster than the output of goods and services.

(2) A related misconception is that it is possible to trade off any given degree of inflation for corresponding levels of unemployment, i.e., that we can purchase whatever level of unemployment we think bearable or desirable by paying the cost in the form of some predictable level of inflation. (This is the famous Phillips Curve hypothesis of recent fame.)

It can be demonstrated that this is true *only* if the specified level of inflation is *unanticipated* by the economic units in the society. Thus an unanticipated rate of inflation of 5 percent may be consistent in a given economy with a 3 percent level of unemployment. But of course a continued rate of inflation of 5 percent soon comes to be anticipated by wage earners, lenders, and others in the economy; this in turn will lead them to demand an inflation premium in their wage rates, interest rates, etc., and the changing cost structure, given *no* change in the rate of increase in the money supply available for spending, would produce reduced outputs and rising unemployment. When this happens, the 5 percent rate of inflation comes to be associated with a much higher rate of unemployment, say 6 percent. To bring the rate of unemployment back to 3 percent would now require an additional and unanticipated inflation factor of (say) another 5 percent, for a total rate of inflation of 10 percent. In other words, as for the drug addict, ever increasing dosages come to be necessary to achieve any given level of "high" or feeling of well-being. Any attempt to maintain unemployment at some given, desired level by the means of a continuously easy money policy must mean not just continuous but accelerating inflation.

(3) Another related misconception can be handled very quickly. It is the belief that the liquidity problems of individuals, businesses, government, and whole nations can be cured by increasing the supply of money within nations and worldwide. An economic unit can be said to face a liquidity problem wherever it can make necessary borrowings only at interest rates that are inconsistent with other parameters in its system, e.g., the family's income available for payments on interest and principal, or the prices the business firm can charge

for its product, or the level of taxation a political unit feels it can impose on its citizens, or the interest payment outflow that a nation's balance-of-payments position would seem to tolerate. The fact is of course that it is inflation itself which tends to produce this seemingly universal illiquidity. Borrowers are tempted to borrow for the very good reason of buying now before prices go even higher; lenders are tempted to lend by the ready insistence of borrowers and the rising charges they can impose on loans. One special feature of this process deserves mention here. In those periods of time when an easy money policy has brought about a temporary lowering of the short-term rate relative to the long-term, those institutions which tend to borrow short and lend intermediate and long tend to expand both their borrowings and their lendings. When the inevitable rise in the short-term rate comes, they then find themselves with a most embarrassing problem of liquidity. At this point they never cease to cry aloud for a new injection of money to save them from a liquidity crunch or crisis. Again the proposed remedy for the ailment turns out to be that which brought the ailment in the beginning and also that which is certain to produce a recurrence of the ailment at a later date.

A liquidity problem, whether it be for Joe Doaks and family, the Widget Manufacturing Company, the First National Bank of Everywhere, the U.S. Government, or the countries of India, England, Italy, and Japan, can never be solved by inflation, by creating more dollars or more pounds or more yen or more SDRs. The temporary relief so gained is purchased at the price of a certain recurrence of the disease, and in a more virulent form.

(4) Another misconception is that inflation is caused by something other than the money relationship and that it can be stopped by doing things other than that of bringing about a proper relationship between the stock of money and the output of goods and services.

One form that this misconception takes is the Keynesion one, the belief that changes in total spending in the economy are not as closely related to changes in the stock of money as to other variables, such as business and consumer propensities and the fiscal actions of governments. For example, in the mid-sixties, the Keynesians who were advising the Johnson administration assumed that in urging a more restrictive fiscal posture on the government, they had taken the important step in fighting the developing inflation and that they could then feel free to recommend a somewhat easy money policy. Although their advice was not followed in all details, the course of action was roughly what they called for—but the consequences were what Friedman and the monetarists were predicting, i.e., rising inflationary pressures under the influence of excessive monetary ease.

Another and more disquieting form that this misconception takes is what might be called the Galbraithian one. It is the belief that inflation is *really* produced through the domino effect of price and wage increases triggered by powerful business, labor, and farm groups in the economy. This point of view is supported neither by common sense nor theory nor the facts. Professor Paul McCracken once said of this idea that "it is still common among uneducated people. Galbraith's view is unusual only in being held by the president of the American Economic Association and in being described by him as new."[1]

It is indicative of the nature of the problem we are facing that this self-same McCracken was to publicly defend a system of wage-price controls instituted by his president just three weeks after he, McCracken, wrote the above statement.

Strong groups within the economy may be able to *divert* spending in various antisocial ways but they cannot bring about an *increase* in total spending, which is what inflation is all about. Trying to stop inflation by wage and price controls is like trying to cure a fever by breaking the thermometer. The observed wage and price increases are but symptoms of the disease. The real problem is the heat in the body economic and this can be reduced only by reducing the rate of increase in the quantity of money.

(5) A final misconception about inflation is that it should be and is possible to stop an inflationary process without cost to anyone in society (except perhaps the

---

[1] *Washington Post,* July 28, 1971.

very rich, who deserve their comeuppance in any case).

The fact is that once inflation lasts for any length of time, it will come to be anticipated in the decisions of a greater part of the society. If inflation is stopped, those anticipations prove to have been in error and the decisions based on those anticipations now have painful consequences: unemployment for the workers who had demanded the higher wages, losses for the firms who had contracted to pay the higher costs, financial loss to all who had purchased assets, directly or indirectly, in anticipation of rising prices, financial distress to all who had borrowed long-term money at high interest rates, etc.

The fact is that we can find not one single case of a society that has been able to stop an inflationary addiction without serious withdrawal pangs, in the form of higher rates of unemployment, lower real output, declining profits, etc. Moreover, the experience indicates that the longer and more rapid the inflationary surge, the more painful the withdrawal process.

The Prophecy

We turn now to my not-so-Delphic forecast of things to come. We have before us most of the ingredients on which I base my specific predictions.

(1) We will have continuing, in fact accelerating inflation in the years ahead. Reasons: (a) It would be

too painful to stop it. Not only would it be painful to many of the citizenry; because it would be painful to the citizenry, it would be political suicide for any administration that really attempted to do it. I am saying that I doubt if any administration could stay in power long enough (or continue to have power enough) to carry through to conclusion a really successful struggle to end inflation. (b) For the same reason, the administrations in power, of whatever political party, will find it necessary to move to a higher rate of inflation from time to time to avoid the letdown that continuing a fully anticipated rate of inflation inevitably brings.

(2) We will *not* have a major depression in the next two decades. No administration could tolerate it, and the alternative (a step-up in the rate of inflation) is much less dangerous, politically, than a major depression. However, because of the imperfect nature of *all* attempts at control and because of the necessity from time to time of taking half-hearted steps to slow down inflation, there will be occasional periods of recession. These will be marked by reduced rates of real growth, perhaps even negative real growth, higher unemployment, etc., *but not by* lowered levels of prices and wages. (The descriptive word is "stagflation"—stagnation with inflation.)

(3) We will have off-and-on wage and price controls. Too many people believe the Galbraith myth, and

the pressure on administrations to do something (or to seem to be doing something) about inflation will bring recurring trials with direct controls. Each new return of controls will be greeted with huzzahs and cheers (even from the business community), only to fall victim to the inevitable frustrations and conflicts of the economic anarchy produced by those controls. Each repeal, though, will leave a larger part of the economy under some form and degree of direct controls.

(4) The combination of continuing (accelerating) inflation and on-again off-again controls will make it increasingly difficult for economic calculation to take place with any degree of efficiency. The subsequent inefficiencies, shortages, frustrations, and inequities will lead to increasing demands for even more detailed control of the private sector. In banking, this may well take the form of governmentally assigned quotas of lending to identified groups and for identified purposes at levels of interest rates well below market. This in turn will mean that the government will itself become an ever more important guarantor of loans and fund source of last resort.

(5) The increasing control of economic life by government can have but one effect on the vitality and strength of the economic process—and that is to sap the vitality and diminish the strength of the most productive economic system in the history of man. With

the size of the pie growing but slowly or diminishing, the conflicts over its division will increase in intensity. As the English experience so clearly demonstrates, these conflicts (particularly in the form of labor disputes) can make the efficient functioning of an integrated economy virtually impossible.

All of this in turn will reduce the capacity of this country to compete in world markets. Our fate, as England's, will then be chronic balance-of-payments problems, continuing loss of faith in the currency in the world money markets, and periodic crises of increasing dimension. If this analysis be at all accurate, then we can say, with Archie the Cockroach, that there is indeed more reason to be optimistic about the past than about the future.

Chapter 2

Alleged Causes of Inflation: Corporate Monopolies

The question before the house is whether inflation is caused, in whole or in part, by the exercise of private market power in the economy. So as to relieve what little suspense there may be, let me hasten to say that the answer to this question is "No." Inflation is not produced by the assistant manager of the A&P store who marks out 43¢ on the can of beans and replaces it with 47¢. Its source is not to be found in the executive offices of the major oil companies—nor even in the exotic, air-conditioned chambers of the oil ministries of the oil producing states of the Third World. Nor is it to be discovered in the admittedly disconcerting, often violent, actions of the minions of George Meany. Even the God of the rainfall, the wind storm, and the wheat rust is blameless of visiting this affliction upon us.

Where, then, must we look if we wish to find those who do in fact control the forces of inflation? To somewhat (but not too seriously) oversimplify, we need look no further than the Open Market Committee of the Board of Governors of the Federal Reserve System. Our fate is determined in the discussions and decisions of this group of reasonably intelligent, eminently well-meaning men of affairs.

Admittedly, these men do not make their momentous decisions in a policy vacuum. As a creature of the legislature, they are operating under certain legislative commands; even more importantly, they are operating in an environment of public opinion, public expectations, and even public clamor. To paraphrase Mr. Dooley, even the Board of Governors of the Federal Reserve System reads the election returns. Thus, if you believe as John Maynard Keynes, Richard Weaver, and I do that ideas do have consequences, that today's public clamor is in large part a product of the academic scribblers of years past, it is necessary to say that Open Market Committee decisions are only the *proximate* cause of the inflationary pressures of the day; the real roots of the problem (and the hopes for its solution as well) are to be found in the cluttered closets where people like John Maynard Keynes, Ludwig von Mises, John Kenneth Galbraith, Walter Heller, Milton Friedman, et al., go about (or have gone about) their work. The regression equations developed by the research staff of the St. Louis Federal Reserve Bank may well be some part of the ammunition that will eventually bring down the walls of the inflationists. In other words, it is ideas, whether right or wrong, that finally count, and one of the most important of the mistaken ideas to be disposed of is the one under discussion here: the idea that market power produces inflation and the corollary policy implication that inflation can be reduced or controlled by direct intervention in wage and price setting.

This call to intellectual and expository activity is really all that I have to pronounce here, but do not think that I shall relinquish the speaker's stand so quickly. My bald, unsubstantiated statements surely require some elaboration—and, in addition, I must at least *seem* to do more to qualify for the modest pay offered to speakers in these meetings.

Market Power and Inflation

The question of the relationship between market power and inflation can be disposed of quickly by definition alone—*if* one accepts what I believe to be the most useful definition of inflation. In the tradition of Mises, I believe the most useful way to define inflation is as a situation in which the quantity of money is increasing more rapidly than the output of goods and services (or, more precisely, than the corresponding need for money). The wage and price increases which tend to follow from this are but the symptoms of the situation itself. Thus, if by draconian measures, all the wage-price-interest rate symptoms of inflation could be suppressed, the inflation would still be present, but its symptoms would be in general (though not universal) shortages of goods and services—in queues before the shops of the butcher, the baker, and the candlestickmaker. As Allen Wallis has pointed out, for the housewife to encounter bare shelves at the fixed price is for her to suffer a fall in the purchasing power of her money just as real as for her to encounter full shelves but at higher prices.

But doesn't the use of market power by large corporations or by small firms acting in concert or by trade unions lead to reduced output of goods and services, thus producing the Mises effect by its impact on the T element in the equation (MV=PT)? In a word, *no*. The exercise of market power can change (in fact, distort) the use of resources from what would have prevailed in the absence of that market power (e.g., fewer workers employed in construction and, because of that, more workers available for other employments). This could lead to some prices (housing, say) being higher than they would otherwise be, but, by the same token, other prices would be lower than they would otherwise be. There is indeed damage to the consumer interest from this state of affairs, but it is a damage different from (and to be corrected by different means than) the damage from inflation. In insisting that the bite of the rattlesnake does not cause cancer, I am not trying to say a kind word for the rattlesnake.

I am only trying to direct the doctor to the correct diagnosis and medication of the ailment.

But suppose one does not accept the Mises approach to defining inflation; suppose one finds it more useful to define inflation as "generally rising prices" or some more precise form of the same idea. Can inflation, so defined, be produced by the exercise of market power? Even with this definition, I would answer in the negative. This definition, by the way, is roughly the one used by most of those who call themselves "monetarists," and who argue as I do that inflation is essentially a monetary phenomenon. Market power may indeed be used to cause some prices or wage rates to be higher than they would otherwise be, but if the total of dollars remains unchanged, this can in turn produce at worst a diverting of dollars from other goods and services, with associated downward pressure on the relevant prices and/or wage rates.

But can't market power at least influence the *lag* between disturbances in M and responses on the price and wage side? There is some evidence that this may indeed happen in some cases, but so what? It is still not the market power that has *produced* the inflation.

Now that I have mentioned "evidence," perhaps I should pay some attention to those of you who prefer something a little more concrete as an answer than warmed-over Mises. I freely admit that I have undertaken no rigorous research of my own on the question under discussion. What I have done is to read the reports from the research of my "betters." Not too surprisingly, what I find there tends to confirm my original presuppositions.

For the single best summary of research findings (including his own) I suggest that you turn to a monograph by Steven Lustgarten of City University of New York, published by that most useful organization, the American Enterprise Institute. The title is *Industrial Concentration and Inflation,* and it includes a forward by Yale Brozen of the University of Chicago, research director of the American Enterprise Institute (and incidentally the man who first turned my own eyes in the direction of market economics).

Brozen summarizes the findings in his foreword as follows:

> It is frequently argued that industries in which a few firms produce most of the output charge higher prices than they would if the large, component firms were broken into several smaller ones (as was done, for example, with the old Standard Oil Company and the American Tobacco Company early in the century). Whether or not the argument is valid, and much evidence to the contrary has appeared, it does not follow that inflation is a consequence of a highly concentrated industrial structure. Assuming, for the sake of argument, that concentrated industries charge higher prices, we should suffer *rising* prices only if industrial concentration were rising. But data for the U.S. economy show average market concentration levels to be fairly stable. That being the case, no connection should be expected between industrial concentration and inflation.

> Professor Lustgarten examines the movement of prices of manufacturing industries. He seeks to determine whether prices in the most concentrated industries increase more rapidly than those in the less concentrated industries. He finds that the price behavior of the highly concentrated industries has not been a source of inflation in the United States. According to his data, the prices of these defamed industries have not only *not* been a source of inflation, but have risen more slowly than those in the atomistic industries. They have, in fact, been a moderating factor in inflation.[1]

Lustgarten's own summary runs as follows:

> Both theoretical and empirical evidence relating industrial concentration to inflation have been examined. The theoretical arguments were that concentration promotes inflation because it allows sellers to maintain prices when demand declines, to pass on inflationary wage increases, and to avoid competitive pressures to reduce costs. These arguments were found to be inconsistent with the evidence, which showed that prices and unit labor costs have increased more slowly in concentrated industries than in other industries.[2]

Admittedly, what Lustgarten and others have done is largely to show that there seems in fact to be no relationship between industrial *concentration* and inflation—and this is not equivalent to proving that there is no relationship between *market power* and inflation.

---

[1] Steven Lustgarten, *Industrial Concentration and Inflation* (Washington, D.C.: American Enterprise Institute, 1975), p. 1.

[2] Ibid., p. 36.

Their findings may only suggest that there is no real relationship between concentration ratios and the real exercise of market power—a thesis I believe to be almost certainly valid.[3]

As a matter of fact, it is my firm conviction that neither concentration ratios nor market shares nor profitability nor any of the usual criteria of imperfectly competitive markets are of any significance to economic performance. To put it another way, I believe that the only meaningful definition of monopoly is that of a position in a market maintained by the use or threat of the use of force. Most commonly, the kind of use of force I have in mind is technically legal, i.e., it comes directly from governmentally enforced barriers to entry or to free market pricing as in plumbing or banking or doctoring or what have you. But it is sometimes in the form of a permissive attitude on the part of those charged with maintaining the peace towards the use of violence by private groups, such as dairy farmers or automobile workers or carpenters.

I intend to return for final comment on this topic in the next section. At the moment I wish to deal with the question of whether or not the exercise of this kind of *real* market power might not be related to inflation. To

---

[3] Here again Brozen is a useful source; see his "Concentration and Profits: Does Concentration Matter?" in Brozen, *The Competitive Economy* (1975).

the disappointment of many of you, I suspect, I must reply that it is my firm belief that not only can Gulf Oil and General Motors not produce inflation but neither can it be "manufactured" in the regulatory offices, the tariff commissions, the city halls, or the courts of the land. Again actions taken (or not taken) there can, like the rattlesnake, introduce a poison into the economic system, but the poison is not that of general inflation.

Here, in part at least, I must disagree with a man whose work I hold in highest esteem, Professor Murray Weidenbaum. Here are his words:

> As the American public is learning to its dismay, there are many ways in which government actions can cause or worsen inflation. Large budget deficits and excessively easy monetary policy are usually cited as the two major culprits, and quite properly. Yet, there is a third, less obvious—and hence more insidious—way in which government can worsen the already severe inflationary pressures affecting the American economy.
>
> That third way is for the government to require actions in the private sector which increase the costs of production and hence raise the prices of the products and services which are sold to the public. . . . Literally, the federal government is continually mandating more inflation via the regulations it promulgates. These actions of course are validated by an accommodating monetary policy.
>
> In theory, the monetary authorities could offset much of the inflationary effects of regulation by attempting to maintain a lower rate of monetary growth. In practice, however,

> public policy makers, insofar as they see the options clearly, tend to prefer the higher rate of inflation to the additional monetary restraint and the resulting decreases in employment and real output.[4]

Weidenbaum notes that the actions he describes require the validating influence of a more rapid rate of increase in the quantity of money to produce their inflationary effects, an admission usually made as well by those who argue that union action does indeed lead to inflation. But here again I would object; if there are no more dollars floating around, the primary effect of government regulation (whether wise or unwise) will be to divert those dollars from one channel to another, with price increases in some areas and price decreases in others, rather than to produce general inflation.

Can Inflation Be Cured by Making the Economy More Competitive?

The heavy emphasis I put upon this point seems to me to be necessary and appropriate. While it is true that the Weidenbaum-type argument may strengthen the case for a long-overdue dismantling of many parts of the regulatory apparatus (a consummation devoutly

---

[4] Murray Weidenbaum, *Government Mandated Price Increases: A Neglected Aspect of Inflation* (Washington, D.C.: American Enterprise Institute, 1975), p. 3.

to be wished), the general argument linking market power to inflation is also being used by such men as Senators Hart and Bayh to propose structural changes in American business that would bring in turn a sharp reduction in the economic well-being of the masses of the people.

As a matter of fact we have been saved from this fate over the years, under the existing legislation, because of a largely tacit recognition by the political leadership of the nation that antitrust makes for great rhetoric but lousy economics. I am absolutely serious when I say to you that I believe the antitrust laws to be in direct opposition to both the spirit and the practice of capitalism. The very criteria by which a businessman measures his success in serving his stockholders and his customers—increasing share of the market, industry leadership, superiority in product and processes over rivals, above-average profitability—are often precisely the same criteria used by the antitrust division of the attorney general's office as evidence of noncompetitive markets. Or, to put it another way, how can we label as "unjust" a position in the market that has been achieved over time through a series of peaceful, nonfraudulent exchanges with willing partners?

It is my firm conviction that Schumpeter was absolutely right when he argued that "the power to exploit at pleasure a given pattern of demand . . . can under the conditions of intact capitalism hardly persist for a period long enough to matter . . . unless buttressed by public authority."[5]

It is my belief that competition inheres in the very nature of man and the exchange economy; in the words of Adam Smith, "All systems of preference or of restraint, therefore, being thus completely taken away, the obvious and simple system of natural liberty establishes itself of its own accord."[6] Competition does not need to be created or protected or restored; all that government need do to see that competition prevails is not to get in its way.

My position here is very similar to that taken by Joseph Schumpeter (and by Mises as well), but I was not brought here to discuss with you the various views on the meaning and nature of competition and monopoly. My assignment was to discuss the question of whether or no the problem of inflation was significantly related to the exercise of market power in the economy.

To summarize, I have argued that market structure and performance are *not* significantly related to the problem of inflation. It follows from this that inflation cannot be reduced or eliminated by actions taken to make the economy more competitive. Moreover, I have insisted that for the nation to turn its policy eyes in

[5] Joseph A. Schumpeter, *Capitalism, Socialism, and Democracy,* 3rd ed. (New York: Harper & Row, 1962), p. 99.

[6] Adam Smith, *The Wealth of Nations* (New York: Modern Library, 1937), p. 651.

that direction would be for it to divert attention from the only area where it must look if it is in fact to bring inflation under control—and, in the process, to be as likely to produce harm as good in the market structures of the economy. Finally I have identified that "only area" where a solution to the problem of inflation is to be found as that of the money supply.

This leaves unresolved all of the really important questions! What is the objective to be sought in the making of monetary policy? No increase in M, however defined? a steady rate of increase? is the proper dial to be watched M_1, or M_2 or M_3? Should all such attempts to create a controlled paper currency be abandoned and replaced by the gold standard? If so, which of the many forms of the gold standard? or should some other commodity standard be put in place?

These are the topics with which other speakers are concerning themselves, and they are not a part of my assignment. However, in closing, I cannot resist offering two comments:

(1) Turning the control of the money supply over to government, under any conditions, is like turning the liquor store over to an alcoholic; and

(2) I do not believe that any expert or group of experts can possibly devise a monetary system as effective as the one that would spontaneously emerge in a

society in which the government played no more and no less of a role with reference to money than I would have it play in all of economic life: maintain law and order, enforce contracts, and stand ready to assist the plaintiff in cases of fraud. In money as elsewhere, I prefer the rule of the market to the rule of men.

Part VII

On the Problems of Cities

The following paper was prepared in response to an invitation in 1972 from the Center for Constructive Alternatives at Hillsdale College to be one of the speakers in a seminar on the general topic, "Recycling the Cities: Alternatives to Decay." I brought to the task little more than a set of ready-made prejudices; not unnaturally, my further studies did little to alter those existing opinions. I am pleased that it did give me an opportunity to pay tribute to a woman whose work I had long admired, Jane Jacobs. I still find in her work a more perceptive handling of the idea of a city than in any other material in this topic area.

Chapter 1

The Problems of Cities

In the paragraphs to follow you will find me critical of most of the work now being done on the nature of the urban crisis and equally critical of the public policies proposed to ease that crisis. To compound my sin, I offer no alternative scheme by which the New Jerusalem can be erected on the shores of the Hudson or Lake Michigan or Lake Erie. I intend to argue that no one even knows how to *define* the New Urban Jerusalem, let alone *construct* it.

In all of this, I will be utilizing no special knowledge of urban processes but rather the simplest of analytical and evaluational concepts of economics. In so doing I am acting upon my firm belief that a handful of hypotheses about human action are sufficient for most, if not all, decisions on economic policy. I would be prepared to argue that the practice of breaking up this useful discipline into agricultural economics, transportation economics, development economics, labor economics, urban economics, etc., has been productive of much mischief. Behind the shield of special circumstances and special knowledge, theories have been developed and given wide acceptance that would be regarded as patently absurd if they were put as a general model; policies have been developed and urged upon society that would be recognizably catastrophic if applied generally.

One Man's Atlantis

Proposition No. 1: The first of the propositions on which I wish to base my argument is the fundamental proposition of all modern value theory: Value does not consist of objectively definable characteristics of a good or service; value exists only as subjective judgment in the mind of each beholder. It cannot be measured directly but only indirectly by the behavior it elicits. There is no way that the subjective valuations of two people can be summed or even directly compared.

Thus, the value of a chair is not something inherently residing in the physical properties of the chair or in its costs of production; its value is different to each viewer and for any one man can be measured only by what other goods or services he would be willing to give up to acquire this particular chair.

There is no way of defining in absolute and universal terms the essential characteristics of the Good Chair; one man's throne is another's torture device. What is true of a chair must be equally true of a city. There is no way of defining in general terms the essential characteristics of the Good City; one man's Atlantis is another's Hell. Nor are there other objective ways of measuring the degree of goodness of a city. For example, it is sometimes argued that a good city is one that survives or one that grows. But as circumstances change, the functions served by a city change, perhaps even disappear. Were some of the ancient cities of history and legend less successful because they no longer exist?

Some illustrations: From the introduction to a recent book with the title *Environment for Man: The Next Fifty Years*, sponsored by the American Institute of Planners:

> If we had the technology and the economy—both said to be imminent—to build an ideal environment, what kind would we build? What could environment contribute to a "good" day? Do we know how to define and work toward "Optimum Environment with Man as the Measure"? To date neither optimum nor environment has been defined, nor have we made an adequate beginning at measuring man. *And we must somehow learn to allow for subjective human values.*[1]

---

[1] *Environment for Man: The Next Fifty Years,* sponsored by the American Institute of Planners, ed. William R. Ewald, Jr. (Bloomington: Indiana University Press, 1967), p. 3.

Here we find repeated the ancient myth of planning, that it is possible both to plan the allocation of resources from the center and also to serve the subjective preference systems of the individuals who make up the society. It is doubtful if the planners are capable of designing programs and processes (even with unlimited funds at their disposal) that will in fact produce the outcomes that they, the planners, desire—to say nothing of the outcomes desired by the other members of the society.

A second illustration: In another recent book with the title, *Sick Cities: Psychology and Pathology,* we find the following:

> The *Saturday Evening Post* in an editorial in 1961 called sprawl "perhaps our cruelest misuse of land since our soil mining days. Urban sprawl," it went on to state, "is not the growth of cities. Instead, the cities are disintegrating and spreading the pieces over miles and miles of countryside."
>
> Robert Moses, responsible for so many of Gothman's public achievements in the present century, takes the opposite point of view in an article in the *Atlantic Monthly:* "The prosperous suburbanite," he says, "is as proud of his ranch home as the owner of the most gracious villa of Tuscany. The little identical suburban boxes of average people, which differ only in color and planting, represent a measure of success unheard of by hundreds of millions on other continents."[2]

[2] Mitchell Gordon, *Sick Cities: Psychology and Pathology* (Baltimore: Penguin Books, 1963), p. 20.

Quick about it: Is "urban sprawl" a vice or a virtue? Well, that all depends. On the basis of my admittedly incomplete reading of the materials in this field, I would conclude that urban sprawl (and all similarly achieved outcomes) are *per se* unacceptable to those who see *any* unplanned outcome as less than optimal. In other words, any characteristic of the urban environment that, like Topsy, "just grew" stands condemned by its very origins.

One final illustration of my thesis, this one drawn from one of the most instructive and civilized books yet written on this topic: *The Death and Life of Great American Cities*, by Jane Jacobs.

> People gathered in concentrations of big-city size and density can be felt to be an automatic—if necessary—evil. This is a common assumption: that human beings are charming in small numbers and noxious in large numbers. Given this point of view, it follows that concentrations of people should be physically minimized in every way: by thinning down the numbers themselves insofar as this is possible, and beyond that by aiming at illusions of suburban lawns and small-town placidity. In follows that the exuberant variety inherent in great numbers of people, tightly concentrated, should be played down, hidden, hammered into a semblance of the thinner, more tractable variety or the outright homogeneity often represented in thinner populations.
>
> On the other hand, people gathered in concentrations of city size and density can be considered a positive good, in the faith that they are desirable because they are the source of immense vitality, and because they do represent,

> in small geographic compass, a great and exuberant richness of differences and possibilities, many of these differences unique and unpredictable and all the more valuable because they are. Given this point of view, it follows that the presence of great numbers of people gathered together in cities should not only be frankly accepted as a physical fact. It follows that they should also be enjoyed as an asset and their presence celebrated.[3]

Quick about it: Is high population density a vice or a virtue? Well, that all depends, As that great, mythical Irish bartender, Mr. Dooley, once put it: "As the Frenchman said, as he drank from the fire extinguisher, 'Each to his own taste.' "

To sum up: Given the fact that value is subjective by its very nature, given the fact of the enormous internal diversity of human populations, and given the never-ending changes in tastes and circumstances, it is impossible *per se* for there to be constructed a universally valid, objective definition or description of the Good City. City planning is by definition, then, an exercise in either futility or coercion (or both).

It *is* possible for a group of people of like values to agree upon a definition of the Good City and to attempt to implement that particular vision with their own monies and without coercion, and to this I offer no objection. But most True Prophets prefer to work with other people's money, obtained by the exertions

---

[3] Jane Jacobs, *The Death and Life of Great American Cities* (New York: Vintage Books, 1961), pp. 220–21.

of the tax collector, and with the sheriff at their side to deal appropriately with those recalcitrant few who stand in the way of the developing New Jerusalem.

Right Rules Promote Right Outcomes

Proposition No. 2: The Good City will be whatever arrangement of things and people emerges out of the decisions of those people when such decisions are made within a framework of appropriate rules. That is to say, *the Good City cannot be defined in terms of its own characteristics but only in terms of the correctness or incorrectness of the decision-system within which it emerges. Right rules promote right outcomes; wrong rules promote wrong outcomes.*

The point that I'm attempting to make here is one I believe to be of greatest significance to this and to all other discussions of social policy-making. I need hardly admit that it is not an idea of my creating but one that many of my betters have developed before me. The best explicit development of this idea, in my opinion, is to be found in the article, "Individualism: True and False," by F. A. Hayek.

> By tracing the combined effects of individual actions, we discover that many of the institutions on which human achievements rest have arisen and are functioning without a designing and directing mind; that, as Adam Ferguson expressed it, "nations stumble upon establishments, which

> are indeed the result of human action but not the result of human design,"[4] and that the spontaneous collaboration of free men often creates things which are greater than their individual minds can ever fully comprehend.[5]

In this and other writings, Hayek points out that this thesis does not imply that good results will flow spontaneously from individual decision-making under any and all institutional frameworks. On the contrary, Hayek and his predecessors have all stressed the necessity of right rules. Here, for example, again from Hayek:

> True Individualism is, of course, not anarchism, which is but another product of the rationalistic pseudo-individualism to which it is opposed. It does not deny the necessity of coercive power but wishes to limit it—to limit it to those fields where it is indispensable to prevent coercion by others and in order to reduce the total of coercion to a minimum.
>
> The most general principle on which an individualist system is based is that it uses the universal acceptance of general principles as the means to create order in social affairs.

He concludes with a sentence that is the stage setting for the rest of this paper.

---

[4] Adam Ferguson, *An Essay on the History of Civil Society,* 1st ed. (1767), p. 187.

[5] F. A. Hayek, "Individualism: True and False," in *Individualism and Economic Order* (Chicago: University of Chicago Press, 1948), pp. 6–8.

> But if our main conclusion is that an individualist order must rest on the enforcement of abstract principles rather than on the enforcement of specific orders, this still leaves open the question of the *kind* of general rules which we want.[6]

Our search, then, is for the right kind of rules, within whose framework the spontaneous forces of social development would work to produce the better city. It is my argument that these rules, in their general form, are to be found not by assigning a team of urban affairs experts to the task but rather by identifying those *general* rules of human conduct that are morally correct and economically efficient. *Note:* Unless the world is totally absurd, that which is correct in principle will also be that which works. It follows from this that those who come closest to understanding and discovering the right principles of human conduct (by whatever means, including, if you wish, revelation) will also come closest to understanding that which will work.

The few simple principles from which I will work from here on out are the ones that make moral sense to me. I need hardly direct your attention to my obvious fallibility and hence to the strong possibility—nay, certainty—that I am wrong in one or all of my presuppositions. I go through this exercise as an illus-

[6] Ibid., p. 19.

tration of what seems to me to be correct procedure—even if the specific principles (and hence answers) are not themselves the correct ones. I remind you that, in my opinion, the correct procedure is one in which, whatever the topic, we reason from first principles to specific policy positions.[7]

You will note that, in doing this, I am careful *not* to attempt to predict the specific details or even the general nature of the outcomes (in terms of urban characteristics) that might flow from the application of the suggested rules to this problem area. The reason, as Hayek has made clear, is that it is impossible to predict the nature of the outcomes of free and peaceful decision-making. Just literally, no one knows what our cities would have looked like had they developed under different rule systems than have in fact prevailed.

What it is possible to do, though, is to relate many of those characteristics of urban life that many see as undesirable to those rule systems that have prevailed—and this I intend to do. This implies that I know what rules would have been morally correct and economically efficient. With a reminder of the caveat issued earlier, I present below a list of some parts of what I consider to be the proper rules system for the dealings of men, one with another, whether those men live in a wilderness or at Broadway and 42nd Street.

---

[7] See Leonard Read, "The Consistent Life," *The Coming Aristocracy* (Irvington, N.Y.: Foundation for Economic Foundation, 1969), pp. 142–49.

1. Individuals and groups shall be permitted (have the right) to enter into voluntary exchanges of goods and services on terms of their own choosing, provided that neither force nor fraud is involved.

2. Individuals and groups shall be permitted (have the right) to use properties legally under their control in any manner they choose, provided that in so doing no damage is inflicted upon the person and/or property of unwilling third parties.

3. The coercive power of government shall not be permitted (has no right) to be used for any purpose other than that of minimizing coercion in human affairs, i.e. for any purpose other than that generally described in the phrase, "law and order."

4. The price to be charged for any good or service shall be that which emerges from the voluntary exchange process.

I am not insisting that this is a complete listing of the appropriate rules. I wish to deal with a manageable number of rules and cases as an illustration of the procedure I believe to be proper, and I do not presume to be presenting a complete, definitive statement of the case.

What I now intend to do is to take each of these four rules and to provide illustrations of specific urban problems that seem to have been brought on or exacerbated by the fact that the rule involved has not been in force.

Rule No. 1: Freedom of Exchange

Case No. 1: I intend to argue here that coercive intervention in labor contracts by government and by labor organizations granted special privileges by government has been an important cause of one of the most dramatic and difficult of the urban problems: the high rate of unemployment among low-productivity work groups in urban areas—the young, the old, minority race members, etc.

Let us begin with minimum wage laws. For the purposes of a book on which I have been working for some time, I have had occasion to examine what I believe to be every major study ever made of the employment effects of minimum wage setting. Most such studies show in one degree or another a significant direct relationship between upward changes in legislated wage minima and increases in the rate of unemployment in low-productivity work groups (with a particularly severe impact on young people from minority race groups).

One of the most informed men in this field, Professor Yale Brozen of the University of Chicago, has written as follows:

> It is hardly surprising that unemployment among the unskilled increased with this rapid rise in the minimum wage.

> To the extent that teenagers are inexperienced, unskilled workers, they are the ones who have been priced out of the labor market by the rise in the minimum wage rate.[8]

That this interpretation of the evidence is not restricted to those identified as conservative economists is attested to by the fact that the Swedish socialist economist and sociologist, Gunnar Myrdal, reports the same kind of finding in his well-known study of American race problems, *An American Dilemma,* where he notes that Negroes have been the main sufferers from the employment effects of minimum wage laws.[9] The distinguished modern liberal economist, Paul Samuelson, asks, "What good does it do a Negro youth to know that an employer must pay him $1.60 per hour, if the fact that he must be paid that amount is what keeps him from getting a job?"[10]

To the problems caused by the minimum wage laws must be added those caused by child labor laws. Senator Abraham Ribicoff has noted that most of the things he did to earn money as a boy would now be forbidden. His conclusion: this country has far too many laws coddling children.[11] Indeed, as many have

---

[8] See Yale Brozen, "Minimum Wage Rates and Household Workers," *Journal of Law and Economics,* V (October 1962): 103–9.

[9] Gunnar Myrdal, *An American Dilemma* (New York: Harper, 1944), p. 297.

[10] Paul Samuelson, *Economics,* 7th ed. (New York: McGraw-Hill, 1967), p. 377.

[11] *Top of the News,* 3 (July 10, 1961): 218.

noted, the great problem of the urban young person is not overwork but a deadening, self-destroying idleness.

Case No. 2: Another one of the critical problems of American cities is the fact that the proportion of blacks in the inner city is increasing dramatically and these blacks do not have ready access to high-income employment and particularly to positions in the skilled trades. This is a topic to be covered in the proposed Rogge book and, in a continuing show of immodesty, I quote again from that source:

> Trade unionism has tended to produce the following consequences on the economic position of the Negro in the American economy: (1) to reduce his access to many of the industries and trades in which trade unionism is an important factor (and particularly in the high-pay, skilled trades) through outright discrimination against nonwhites; (2) to reduce the opportunities for the Negro to move to the higher-paid skilled or supervisory positions, again through outright discrimination; and (3) to reduce generally the opportunities for the Negro to find employment in union-covered industries and trades through (a) the raising of wage rates above what the market would have brought into being, and (b) the insistence on equal pay for equal work. Admittedly, some Negroes have shared in the higher incomes associated with union pressures on employers; on balance, though, the Negro has probably been a significant loser from the growth and present strength of trade unionism in the American economy.[12]

[12] Benjamin A. Rogge, unpublished manuscript.

The same point has been made by Sir Arthur Lewis, the Jamaican-born black economist (and socialist) now teaching at Princeton University, who has written recently, "The trade unions are the black man's greatest enemy in the United States."[13]

To summarize: some of the problems usually identified as afflicting the city relate to the high unemployment rates in the low-productivity work groups in the city and to the difficulty of minority race group members moving into the higher-paid, higher-skill jobs. I have argued that both of these urban problems have arisen in part from coercive interventions in the labor-exchange process by agencies of government and by private groups granted semi-governmental privileges.

As Vic Fingerhut, once principal speechwriter for Vice-President Hubert Humphrey, has pointed out, one of the central economic functions of the American city over the decades has been as a locus of relatively low-cost labor supplies. This was reflected in the great variety of light manufacturing, service, and labor-intensive industries that were to be found in the cities of this country.

As artificial restrictions have been imposed upon the labor market, the city has produced unhappy consequences for urban populations.

> Welfare legislation, minimum wages, maximum work hours, and the like have minimized the economic function

[13] *Chicago Tribune,* May 11, 1969, p. 2.

> of the conglomerations of poor-but-willing people in our cities. Similarly, the goad of hunger has been mitigated by the rising level of welfare payments. In Newark a woman with three children lives very badly on welfare payments, but these nevertheless average somewhere around $300 to $350 per month. To live at the same level, a man with a wife and three children would have to make about $5,500 a year. For unskilled labor, that sort of money just isn't available.[14]

This factor also accounts in part for the high welfare costs of most cities today—and for the high living costs in urban areas. A city can function only as it uses a high ratio of service-oriented industries not called for in the countryside, and it is precisely such services that are made much more expensive as a result of wage interventions.

Some of the market interventions that damage urban dwellers deal not with city processes but with farm processes. Thus the whole of the American farm program, including milk marketing programs and the whole paraphernalia of price supports and output restriction, impinges unfavorably on the urban consumer. Its impact is particularly severe on the low-income urban consumer because he spends a very large part of his income on food, fiber, and alcohol—all derived in whole or in part from farm outputs.

In one market after another, in one interference with

[14] George Sternlieb, "The City as Sandbox," *The Public Interest,* 25 (Fall 1971): 17.

voluntary exchange after another, the state has added to the woes of urban America. The policy implications would seem to be obvious.

Rule No. 2: Property Rights and Control

Individuals and groups shall be permitted (have the right) to use properties legally under their control in any manner they choose, provided that in so doing no damage is inflicted upon the person and/or property of unwilling third parties.

This would seem to be a two-part rule. Part 1 deals with the bundle of rights known as "Private property," while part 2 deals with the problem usually identified as "pollution" or "externalities" or "neighborhood effects." In fact they are two sides of the same coin. A's right to use his property as he sees fit cannot be used as a defense of an action of his which denies B *his* right to *his,* B's property. The freedom of your fist ends at my nose; the freedom to use private property ends at the property line. Spillovers from A's actions that affect B's use of his property are a direct violation of the right of property.

It should be obvious to one and all that modern governments have sinned grievously in both aspects of this private property rule. They have themselves invaded the property of private citizens in a great variety of ways, and they have not protected the property rights of the B's of this world from the unwanted intrusions of the A's.

In what ways have governments in cities (and elsewhere) invaded the property rights of their citizens? In many, many ways. An example would be the use of the weapon of eminent domain to confiscate private properties for use by the state or for use by other private persons or groups. Is a road to be built? Seize the property of the citizen, paying him a price for it that, had he been willing to accept, would have made the confiscation unnecessary. Is it decided that some collection of assets is unsightly and undesirable? Seize those assets, tear down the buildings, then make the land available to other private parties and at a price by definition lower than they would have had to pay in a truly voluntary exchange. This is known as urban renewal or city planning or what-have-you.

If you wish to understand the true consequences of such actions, read the Martin Anderson book, *The Federal Bulldozer,*[15] or the following pages from the Jane Jacobs book:

> There is a wistful myth that if only we had enough money to spend—the figure is usually put at a hundred billion dollars—we could wipe out all our slums in ten years, reverse decay in the great, dull, gray belts that were yesterday's and day-before-yesterday's suburbs, anchor the

[15] Martin Anderson, *The Federal Bulldozer* (Cambridge: MIT Press, 1964).

wandering middle class and its wandering tax money, and perhaps even solve the traffic problem.

But look what we have built with the first several billions: Low-income projects that become worse centers of delinquency, vandalism and general social hopelessness than the slums they were supposed to replace. Middle-income housing projects which are truly marvels of dullness and regimentation, sealed against any buoyancy or vitality of city life. Luxury housing projects that mitigate their inanity, or try to, with a vapid vulgarity. Cultural centers that are unable to support a good bookstore. Civic centers that are avoided by everyone but bums, who have fewer choices of loitering places than others. Commercial centers that are lack-luster imitations of standardized suburban chain-store shopping. Promenades that go from no place to nowhere and have no promenaders. Expressways that eviscerate great cities. This is not the re-building of cities. This is the sacking of cities.

That such wonders may be accomplished, people who get marked with the planners' hex signs are pushed about, expropriated, and uprooted much as if they were the subjects of a conquering power. Thousands upon thousands of small businesses are destroyed, and their proprietors ruined, with hardly a gesture at compensation. Whole communities are torn apart and sown to the winds, with a reaping of cynicism, resentment and despair that must be heard and seen to be believed.[16]

Explicit Ownership, No Zoning

In the same way that it has itself violated B's property rights, the state has permitted, in one form

[16] Jacobs, *Great American Cities,* pp. 4–5.

or another, to one degree or another, the A's of the world to trespass on B's property through air pollution, noise, etc. It is not that laws have not existed dealing with such questions. Indeed, that most remarkable of the unplanned creations of Western man, the common law, included a long history of cases in which the courts had redressed B's grievances against the trespassing A's of the world. (See for example, an unpublished doctoral dissertation by my colleague at Wabash, Steven Schmutte.)[17]

In many cities the general welfare was thought to require that the A's (perhaps major employing firms in the area) be permitted to continue to trespass on the properties of the B's in the community, else they might leave and set up shop in another city.

Admittedly, once a firm has been permitted to pollute for many years, a kind of adverse possession problem arises, and equity may demand an appropriate time period for a remedy to be developed. Moreover, it is inefficient and inappropriate for the court to state precisely *what form* the remedy is to take. To the charge that this is going to "cost a great deal," I reply that the cost is already being assessed—but it is being assessed in part against innocent third parties. The cost should be borne by the users of the goods and

---

[17] "Interrelations of Law and Economics: The Case of Stream Pollution," Ph.D. diss., Purdue, 1971.

services involved, not by unwilling recipients of smoke, irritants, and noise.

I might add that the proper approach is not to proscribe certain activities (such as brick-making) in certain areas, but to proscribe the externalities. If a firm can find a way to make bricks in the center of an affluent suburb in such a way as to produce no externalities, no damage to surrounding properties, and if this is what it believes to be the appropriate site for the activity, the state should not intervene—as it now does with its zoning laws. The city of Houston, Texas, has demonstrated the practicability of a city operating without zoning laws. Such laws represent an unwarranted invasion of private property and are certain to be abused by the governments involved.

A substantial part of the problem of externalities relates to the choice of uses for "spaces" (such as the air, lakes and streams, oceans, etc.) to which no one has explicit ownership. The Tragedy of the Commons arose precisely because it *was* a commons and not the private property of any one person or group. Should a given pond of water be used for boating or for fishing or as a wild game preserve or as a focal point for home sites or as a source of a cooling agent for a generating plant? Permit private ownership of the lake and such questions are readily resolved by the simple process of competitive bidding. And if the people of the city, who want more electric power, outbid the fishermen, so be it. As such questions are now decided, a few hundred (upper-income?) fishermen and nature lovers may be able to secure the lake as a fishing reserve at no cost to themselves and even persuade the state to provide the fish as well.

This has been a most hurried and oversimplified look at a difficult problem area. But the difficulty lies not in deciding the proper principles to apply; the difficulty lies in the details of working out the applications of the principle.

To summarize: Through sins of both commission and omission, governments at all levels have violated the principle of private property. Some of the serious problems of urban America seem to arise from precisely the fact that states have themselves invaded private property and have permitted one private citizen to invade the property of another, in the form of spillover effects. Again, the policy implications seem obvious.

Rule No. 3: Only Minimize Coercion

The coercive power of government shall not be permitted (has no right) to be used for any purpose other than that of minimizing coercion in human affairs, i.e. for any purpose other than that generally described in the phrase, "law and order."

Here again governments at all levels have been involved in sins of commission and omission. They have undertaken a whole host of activities that have nothing to do with minimizing coercion, and at the same time they have done a rather poor job in this country of maintaining law and order.

Governments are involved in owning and operating schools, hospitals, utilities, housing projects, parks, golf courses, airports—but the list is almost limitless. In addition they subsidize, regulate, supervise, and harass private owners and operators of enterprises.

It is my firm conviction that it can be demonstrated that these departures from right principle have produced unwanted rather than wanted outcomes. I believe it can be demonstrated that many of what are said to be the great problem areas of urban America—housing, transportation, school systems, tax burdens, etc.—are directly traceable to overextension of government's role in human affairs.

I would find it interesting and useful to take but one of these areas—say, hospitals or schools—and attempt to prove my point. In fact, I have done just this for higher education and have come to the conclusion that "tax-supported education tends to make of our schools and colleges a collection of nonstudents under the tutelage of nonteachers and the administration of the incompetent."[18] However, time will not permit any fuller exploration of this and related topics. Suffice it to say that it is precisely the areas where the

---

[18] See Part VIII, Chapter 1, below.

state has stepped in that problems of quality, quantity, and cost are most in evidence; those goods and services relatively untouched by the dead hand of the state are precisely the ones about which we need not be concerned.

This disease of overextended government seems to strike urban areas more severely than rural (although God knows it is not unknown in the latter). One of the more obvious consequences of this fact is the constantly rising tax burdens that must then be imposed on urban populations. This in turn prompts both private citizens and businesses to escape the city, thus reducing the tax base, increasing welfare costs, etc., which in turn calls for even higher tax rates, and so on. The great multiplication of governmental activities has taken both attention and funds from the one legitimate area for government action: law and order. City planners seem always to be better paid than city policemen.

Nonmarket Pricing of Services

We turn now to the consequences that flow from the fact that many of the services offered within and around the city are not priced in a market process.

Example: One of the more dramatic examples is to be found in the transportation services in urban areas.

Specific users may be charged nothing or may pay a charge having little or nothing to do with the costs of providing the facility. This distorts the decision-making of both those who use and those who provide the facilities involved.

Here is the way in which Dean Dick Netzer of New York University's School of Public Administration, chairman of the Inter-University Committee on Urban Economics, has described some typical cases:

> There have been a number of estimates of the full social costs involved in peak-hour use of high-capacity urban freeways to and from the CBD. One such estimate is that the costs commonly exceed 11 cents per vehicle-mile. Ordinarily, the only prices for specific trips on highways that motorists confront are the gasoline taxes they pay, amounting to no more than 1 cent per vehicle-mile. So the peak-hour motorist should really be paying a price for highway use which is ten (or more) times greater than the price he usually does pay, while the peak-hour transit rider's fare should rise by much smaller proportions.
>
> For the latter, an extreme case—for example, the construction of a new subway line in New York City to relieve overcrowding—might require a three- or four-fold increase in the fare. For peak-hour motorists, the extreme cases are truly fantastic. For example, if peak-hour uses of the proposed third tube of the Queens-Midtown Tunnel in New York, required only for rush-hour traffic, had to pay its full costs, the indicated toll would be at least $5, compared to 25 cents at present.[19]

[19] Netzer, op. cit., pp. 143–44.

In describing the impact of such pricing practices on city characteristics, Netzer concludes as follows:

> Thus, the highly dispersed form of residential development characteristic of most American urban areas, involving heavy auto use even for commuting to work is not necessarily independent of changeable transportation characteristics. If auto use were no longer faster, more comfortable, and cheaper, it is a fair bet that some consumers would choose other transport modes and some of these would alter their residential location choices as well.

In a longer, more complete demonstration, a wider range of rules and cases could be explained. For example, no study of the city should be thought complete that ignores the consequences that have come from the modern system of welfare. The appropriate rule of right principle would be one that speaks against any coerced transfer of assets from one person to another. The case would build upon the incredible problems that have come from the impact of state welfare availability in urban areas upon the social, political, and economic faces of the city. But enough is enough. It is time to summarize.

Summary: Toward the Good City

I have argued that, given the subjective, individual nature of value, it is impossible *per se* for there to be created a single, objective, meaningful definition or description of the Good City. I have questioned whether it would be possible by any means whatsoever to construct such a city, even were it possible to define it in advance.

I have presented as my central thesis the idea that the Good City cannot be described or aimed at in terms of its own characteristics but only in terms of the rightness of the rules system within which it emerges. Again, right rules promote right outcomes; wrong rules promote wrong outcomes.

I have admitted (nay, insisted) that the exact nature of the outcomes that would flow from right rules cannot be predicted in advance. I have insisted, though, that it is possible to identify kinds of generally admitted city ills that have been brought on by wrong rules. The greater part of the paper has consisted of case studies of this part of the argument.

Let me close with a summarizing example of what I am trying to say. This, too, is drawn from the book by Jane Jacobs, *The Death and Life of Great American Cities,* and it relates to the "grew-like-Topsy" evolution of a given section of the city of Boston.

> Twenty years ago, when I first happened to see the North End, its buildings—town houses of different kinds and sizes converted to flats, and four- or five-story tenements built to house the flood of immigrants from Ireland, then from Eastern Europe and finally from Sicily—were badly overcrowded, and the general effect was of a district taking a terrible physical beating and certainly desperately poor.

When I saw the North End again in 1959, I was amazed at the change. Dozens and dozens of buildings had been rehabilitated. Instead of mattresses against the windows there were Venetian blinds and glimpses of fresh paint. Many of the small, converted houses now had only one or two families in them instead of the old crowded three or four. Some of the families in the tenements (as I learned later, visiting inside) had uncrowded themselves by throwing two older apartments together, and had equipped these with bathrooms, new kitchens and the like. Mingled all among the buildings for living were an incredible number of splendid food stores, as well as such enterprises as upholstery making, metal working, carpentry, food processing. The streets were alive with children playing, people shopping, people strolling, people talking.

I could not imagine where the money had come from for the rehabilitation, because it is almost impossible today to get any appreciable mortgage money in districts of American cities that are not either high-rent, or else imitations of suburbs. To find out, I went to a bar and restaurant and called a Boston planner I know.

"Why in the world are you down in the North End?" he said. "Money? Why, no money or work has gone into the North End. Nothing's going on down there. Eventually, yes, but not yet. That's a slum!"

"It doesn't look like a slum to me," I said.

"Why, that's the worst slum in the city. It has two hundred and seventy-five dwelling units to the net acre! I hate to admit we have anything like that in Boston, but it's a fact."

"Do you have any other figures on it?" I asked.

"Yes, funny thing. It has among the lowest delinquency, disease, and infant mortality rates in the city. It also has the lowest ratio of rent to income in the city. Boy, are those people getting bargains. Let's see . . . the child pop-

> ulation is just about average for the city, on the nose. The death rate is low, 8.8 per thousand, against the average city rate of 11.2. The TB death rate is very low, less than 1 per ten thousand, can't understand it, it's lower even than Brookline's. In the old days the North End used to be the city's worst spot for tuberculosis, but all that has changed. Well, they must be strong people. Of course, it's a terrible slum."
>
> "You should have more slums like this," I said. "Don't tell me there are plans to wipe this out. You ought to be down here learning as much as you can from it."
>
> "I know how you feel," he said. "I often go down there myself just to walk around the streets and feel that wonderful, cheerful street life. Say, what you ought to do, you ought to come back and go down in the summer if you think it's fun now. You'd be crazy about it in summer. But of course we have to rebuild it eventually. *We have got to get those people off the streets.*"[20]

I submit that the problem lies in the attitude expressed in that last sentence. The solution lies in a return to those principles of human conduct that are generally and universally valid, in fact, to the ancient principles of private property, limited government and individual freedom.

[20] Jacobs, *Great American Cities,* pp. 9–10.

Part VIII

On Education

I served as academic dean of Wabash College from 1956 through August 1964. The college somehow survived the pervasive aura of disorganization that marks my administrative style and, in the meantime, I came under the necessity of doing some concentrated thinking on various issues in higher education. The two papers in this section are samples drawn from that thinking.

The first paper ("Financing Higher Education") was prepared for a meeting of the Mont Pelerin Society in Switzerland in 1957. A year or two later it was shortened and published in the *Wall Street Journal*. The response of my colleagues on campuses around the country was, shall we say, heated.

The second ("The Promise of the College") was given most recently in 1972 as a commencement address at Park-Tudor, a private school in Indianapolis.

Chapter 1

Financing Higher Education in the United States

The purpose of this study is to explore certain current and expected problems in the financing of higher education in the United States. In particular, it will be directed to an evaluation of one method of solving these problems: the method of full-cost pricing of the services of higher education.[1]

The central thesis of this paper is that full-cost pricing has much to recommend it, both as a solution to the pressing financial problems of higher education and as a solution to other serious problems flowing from below-cost pricing. It is argued that the traditional reasons advanced to support the need for subsidy to higher education, even if accepted, do not

---

1 The findings may or may not be relevant to elementary and secondary education. At the very least, this relevance would have to be established by a study specifically directed to those two stages in the educational process.

demand below-cost pricing as the method of subsidy. A secondary thesis is that the case for subsidy has itself been both exaggerated and distorted and requires careful reexamination.

Statement of the Problem

No time need be spent here establishing the fact that the colleges and universities of this country, both public and private, do indeed face a serious financial problem. This is one of the best publicized facts in the United States today. In sum, the story is that of an industry which confronts a financial crisis because of a fast-rising demand for its services.

This statement of the problem is used deliberately to throw in sharp relief the unique character of the industry. It is one in which the service is sold for much less than its cost of production.[2] It is this and this only which makes of an increase in demand a matter of deep concern rather than a reason for optimism. An increase in the size of a student body usually means a larger deficit—a deficit that must be financed through public and/or private subsidy.

To most students of the problem (including most

[2] A study of various collections of data reveals that the revenues from tuition charges cover from 15 percent to 25 percent of the costs at publicly controlled institutions and from 45 percent to 55 percent of the costs at privately controlled institutions.

college and university presidents) the problem is simply one of raising more money to meet the larger deficits. To only a few does it seem to be reason for a careful and thorough reexamination of the nature and purposes of higher education and of the financial arrangements most likely to promote those purposes. It is the thesis of this study that such a reexamination is badly needed. In particular, to view the problem as simply a desperate need for expanded subsidy to higher education is to ignore the many problems that are associated with below-cost pricing—problems that will not be solved even if the expanded subsidy is secured.

Note: This study is designed to concentrate attention on how educational services are *priced,* not on how the buyers of those services secure the funds to pay the prices asked. That is, full-cost pricing does not rule out private and/or public subsidies to individual students. There are really two questions here: One is how the service should be priced, and the other is who should ultimately bear the cost of the service. Both will be examined, but the first will receive the more careful study.

The Effect of Below-Cost Pricing on Higher Education

To subject higher education to economic analysis may seem to be laying profane hands on a sacred symbol. Such is the mystique of this industry that it must not be appraised with the vulgar calculus of the market-place.

Yet "the vulgar calculus of the market place" still remains as the most humane method man has yet devised to solve those problems of allocation and division which are ubiquitous and permanent in human society. This we have accepted as a people by our continued commitment to the free market form of economic organization. We profess our faith in this form of economic organization for the economy at large, but deny that it is suited to the purposes of higher education. Free market pricing is deemed appropriate for most goods and services, but is rejected in pricing the services of higher education. The reasons advanced to support this position will be examined, but attention will be directed first to certain effects of this policy on the educational system itself. The question to be examined can be phrased in this way: How does below-cost pricing affect the college and university system of this country?

The impact of below-cost pricing on higher education will be examined under four headings: *problems of finance, problems of rationing, problems of motivation,* and *problems of educational efficiency.*

Problems of Finance

To most observers the *only* problem presented by below-cost pricing is the financial problem—the deficits that must be underwritten by the taxpayer or the private donor. Admittedly the financial problem is a serious one. This fact is clearly evidenced in the increasing tendency for college and university presidents (even of tax-supported institutions) to be fund-raisers first and educational leaders and scholars second.

The college or university president must of necessity be a professional beggar, and the pressure of performing in this role is undoubtedly one of the factors leading to the rapid turnover of presidents in American colleges and universities.

The financial problem presented by below-cost pricing *is* a serious one and is rapidly becoming a problem of fantastic proportions. Given the fact of below-cost pricing, there seems to be no solution to this problem that does not involve a significant increase in the burden of the taxpayer. Nor does it seem likely that it will be eased without ever-increasing reliance on funds supplied by the federal government.

Problems of Rationing

But the financial problem is not the only problem presented by below-cost pricing, nor is it even necessarily the most serious. At least as serious is the rationing problem which comes from selling educational services at well below the price which would clear the market.

The price of a good or service in a free market is not only a source of funds to cover the costs of the good or service. It is also the instrument which answers the question of to whom the available supply is to go. That is, price *rations* the total number of units available among those who wish to buy the product. It does this on the principle that the product is to go to those who are willing to give up the most (i.e., pay the highest price) to obtain it.

The acceptability of this principle need not be debated here. It is important only to note that it is one device for rationing. Moreover, it is a device that clears the market and that operates without any need for the seller to choose among buyers on some personal basis.

To set a price below the market price is to create an excess of quantity demanded over quantity supplied, whether the product be sirloin steak, rental housing, or education. This in turn requires of the seller that he find some way to determine whose requests for the product are to be granted and whose denied.

The problem of rationing the available educational services is fast becoming one of the major problems of higher education. This has brought into sharp relief the issue of the rationing principle to be used. The generally accepted principle is that educational opportunities are to go to those possessed of the greatest potential for intellectual growth. This principle has an immediate rationale in that education certainly involves intellectual activity. But closer examination reveals that it can be questioned on both practical and theoretical grounds.

If the principle is accepted, the first task is to *mea-*

sure potential for success in college. No one who has served on the admissions committee of a college or university would argue that this is a simple task. On the contrary, it is one of the most difficult tasks of college administration. Techniques for measuring potential are being improved each year, but mistakes are still made and will continue to be made under the best of measurement programs.

Somewhat less difficult, but no less trying, is the task of determining which students are to be permitted to continue in school, once admitted, and which are to be denied further access to the services of higher education.

The rationing technique under discussion here—whether applied in the selection of students for admission or in the selection of those to continue—operates in such a way that it often appears to the rejected student as a personally discriminatory technique. The rationing system of the free market at least has the advantage of operating as does the system of justice represented by the blindfolded goddess holding the scales. It does not ask "Who are you?" or "What kind of person are you?" or "Did your mother or father attend this college?" but only "Are you willing to pay the price?" Cruel as this may sometimes seem in practice, it would appear on balance to be less cruel and less humiliating than the personalized techniques of nonmarket rationing.

But even if potential for intellectual growth and general success in college could be measured with complete accuracy and in such a way as to leave no room for personally discriminatory decisions, there would still exist serious questions of the appropriateness of this principle. It seems to rest on the assumption that large jars should be filled with the purest wine, while smaller jars should receive nothing but such rainwater as they can catch from the skies. If education is opportunity for personal growth, are we to deny it in some arbitrary way to those unfortunate enough to start from a lower level or to possess less absolute capacity for growth? Is 30 percent growth for the bright student more to be preferred than 30 percent growth for the less able student?

Is it not possible that the brighter student is more capable of educating himself than the weaker student; that in fact it might not be nonsense to say to the quick-minded student, "Go educate yourself," and to the less-gifted student, "Come, we will try to help you"? As a matter of fact, current practice on United States campuses is moving toward independent study programs for the gifted students—a back-handed recognition of the fact that to such students the traditional apparatus of the college may not be important. This is not to argue that admission should be limited to the *poor* student, but only to indicate that the principle that admission should be limited to the good student can be questioned.

Suppose this same principle of making educational opportunities available only to those with high potential to benefit from those opportunities were applied to other goods and services. The sale of opera tickets would then be restricted to those who could establish ability to enjoy opera. Wine would be sold only to the recognized connoisseur, and most wives would be denied the privilege of attending baseball games with their husbands.

For almost all other goods and services we assume that the individual is the best judge of whether or not he is receiving his money's worth. Only in education do we give to the seller the power to make this decision for the buyer.

It might be answered that this is made necessary by the fact that college students are too immature to make this decision for themselves. This answer ignores the fact that the family of the college student participates in this decision and that we permit this same family to make most other decisions for the children in the family. Why is the family less able to make decisions about education than about medical care or clothing or housing for the members of the family?

In sum, the rationing principle in current use in higher education in the United States today is questionable in both philosophy and in practice. Yet below-cost pricing makes some such arbitrary and capricious method of rationing a necessity.

Note: College faculties usually give enthusiastic endorsement to this rationing principle. Could this be because they find it easier and more pleasant to interest the already interested, to seem to produce growth in those destined to grow anyway? This is an understandable feeling, but it seems something less than sufficient as a justification for the principle.

Problems of Motivation

Under the price system, a unit of any given product goes to the one who is willing to give up the most to get it. This is a rationing principle which tends in part to be a measure of strength of motivation. It tends to weed out those who have no great interest in the product. The effect of far-below-cost pricing in higher education is to admit many who have no strong desire to be educated—thus, the curious situation exists in which professors and deans must be constantly belaboring students to take that which they profess to desire. We are in the position of a grocer who must keep close watch on his customers to see that they do not pay for the merchandise and then try to get out of the store without it.

But the effect on the motivation of teachers is equally significant. To the extent that their incomes come from sources other than student fees, they are freed from some part of the necessity to really attend to the interests and wishes of the students. It is curious how irritated teachers become at any suggestion that their product be evaluated by their customers. They really seem to desire that each teacher be judge in his own cause, or at worst that he be judged by his colleagues (who of course should not be so vulgar as to consult student opinion of his work as a teacher).

A number of the points under discussion here are well made in Adam Smith's *Wealth of Nations*. Smith comments on the effect of divorcing teacher income from student fees as follows:

> In other universities, the teacher is prohibited from receiving any honorary or fee from his pupils, and his salary constitutes the whole of the revenue which he derives from his office. His interest is, in this case, set as directly in opposition to his duty as it is possible to set it. It is the interest of every man to live as much at his ease as he can; and if his emoluments are to be precisely the same, whether he does or does not perform some very laborious duty, it is certainly his interest, at least as interest is vulgarly understood, either to neglect it altogether, or, if he is subject to some authority which will not suffer him to do this, to perform it in as careless and slovenly a manner as that authority will permit. If he is naturally active and a lover of labour, it is his interest to employ that activity in any way from which he can derive some advantage, rather than in the performance of his duty, from which he can derive none.
>
> If the authority to which he is subject resides in the body corporate, the college, or university, of which he himself is a member, and in which the greater part of the other members are, like himself, persons who either are, or ought to be teachers, they are likely to make a common cause, to be all very indulgent to one another, and every man to

> consent that his neighbour may neglect his duty, provided he himself is allowed to neglect his own. In the university of Oxford, the greater part of the public professors have, for these many years, given up altogether even the pretence of teaching.[3]

He then comments on the effect of loss of student control in the choice of teachers:

> If in each college, the tutor or teacher, who was to instruct each student in all arts and sciences, should not be voluntarily chosen by the student, but appointed by the head of the college; and if, in case of neglect, inability, or bad usage, the student should not be allowed to change him for another, without leave first asked and obtained; such a regulation would not only tend very much to extinguish all emulation among the different tutors of the same college, but to diminish very much, in all of them, the necessity of diligence and of attention to their respective pupils. Such teachers, though very well paid by their students, might be as much disposed to neglect them, as those who are not paid by them at all or who have no other recompense but their salary. . . .
>
> The discipline of colleges and universities is in general contrived, not for the benefit of the students, but for the interest, or, more properly speaking, for the ease of the masters. Its object is, in all cases, to maintain the authority of the master, and whether he neglects or performs his duty, to oblige the students in all cases to behave to him as if he performed it with the greatest diligence and ability. It seems to presume perfect wisdom and virtue in the one order, and the greatest weakness and folly in the other. Where the masters, however, really perform their duty,

[3] Adam Smith, *The Wealth of Nations* (New York: Modern Library, 1937), pp. 717–18.

> there are no examples, I believe, that the greater part of the students ever neglect theirs. No discipline is ever requisite to force attendance upon lectures which are really worth the attending, as is well known wherever any such lectures are given.[4]

In sum, then, while the student may find it pleasant to have his education subsidized, the price he pays for this is loss of control over his education. He who pays the piper will call the tune, and if the student is not the one who pays the piper, he cannot call the tune. Moreover, the divorce of teacher income from student fees has a tendency to encourage inefficient and ineffective teaching and to encourage teachers to treat their teaching duties as a necessary evil to be disposed of as quickly as possible so as to permit them more time for more important activities. An exaggeration? Perhaps, but who can say that he has never seen such tendencies at work?

The small, private colleges have the reputation of providing the best quality of teaching in higher education. Why is this? Might it have a connection with the fact that such institutions derive 50 percent or more of their revenues from student fees? Thus, the quality of the teaching has an important effect on the revenues of the college, and the administration is forced to encourage and demand of its faculty a high quality of teaching service.

In sum, the effect of below-cost pricing is to make of

---

[4] Ibid., pp. 719–20.

our colleges a collection of students, many of whom have no real desire to make use of the opportunity and a collection of teachers who are under no real necessity to provide a high quality of teaching services.

Problems of Educational Efficiency

The problems to be examined here are usually discussed under the heading of Problems of Academic Freedom. However, academic freedom is really a misnomer. It should not be confused with freedom in the sense of those rights which are guaranteed to Americans in the Bill of Rights. It is altogether fitting and proper that a person should be free to worship as he pleases (or not to worship at all), to think as he pleases, to speak and write as he pleases *without fear of reprisal by government*. In fact, these rights are the very cornerstone of the free society, and they are literally worth dying for.

But to say that Paul Robeson should be free to sing the Communist Internationale is a far different thing from saying that we must pay him for singing the Communist Internationale. We may believe that William Z. Foster should be free to publish books on the communist line, but we are not violating his freedom when we refuse to buy them. Now perhaps we are missing a chance to become better educated by refusing to buy them, and that brings us to the point here. So-called academic freedom is really a question of educational efficiency, of the improved understanding which comes from being exposed to a variety of points of view.

No teacher has an inherent right to present a point of view and to be paid for presenting it. If his customers wish not to pay to hear his point of view, this may be unwise on their part, but it is not a violation of any inherent freedom. In fact, to force them through the taxing power of the government to pay a teacher to present a point of view which they do not wish presented is a violation of an important freedom—the freedom of each man to spend his money as he pleases. Consider, for example, the injustice that would be done if the trustees of a college which demands acceptance of the Apostle's Creed as a condition of employment, were to be forced to hire or to continue to employ an acknowledged atheist, in the interest of academic freedom. Or if a Quaker college were forced to hire General Mark Clark as its president.

But insisting that what is called academic freedom does not really involve freedom is not to minimize its importance. On the contrary, even though it is really a question of educational efficiency, is a very important question. It *is* important that students be given an opportunity to hear and read a variety of points of view, particularly on questions of social policy. In the words of John Stuart Mill, "There is always hope when people are forced to listen to both sides; it is when they attend only to one side that errors harden into prejudices."

This brings us back finally to the matter of below-cost pricing. The necessity for finding funds to fill the gap between student fees and total costs is always potentially dangerous to the integrity of an institution, to its continued ability to offer a program which embraces a wide range of social philosophies and which is otherwise educationally efficient.

The reasoning runs as follows: While the piper must inevitably be subject to pressure from those who pay him, his opportunity to play a varied and personally satisfying concert is greater the more numerous the sources of his support and the less dependent he is upon the support of one payer or one group of payers. In other words, his best protection lies in a wide diffusion of the economic power which he confronts. For example, if an institution becomes dependent on a government for support, the government will be strongly tempted to call the tunes. This control can and has been used to dictate not only the "proper" social philosophies for teachers but the "proper" content of the curriculum as well. Even the assumption that the government is controlled by majority vote of the citizenry is cold consolation to an institution that prefers the point of view of the minority.

In the same way, for a private college to become dependent on a few men of wealth, or on a relatively homogeneous alumni body or on corporation giving, is to create a potential for control and dictation. Of course, a mixing of all of these with student fees does provide considerable diffusion of power, and this is the real strength of the private college as compared to the public. But even this mixing may leave a few men or a few corporations in a position to wield extraordinary influence on the policies of the college.

Note: It must be insisted that there is no violation of inherent right if these men or corporations insist on exerting the influence they possess. They have helped to pay the piper, and they have a right to call some of the tunes. But this is a situation in which the educational efficiency of the institution may not be maximized. Now sometimes these money-givers from among the Philistines have a better idea of what the college should be doing than does the faculty and administration. But there is no reason to believe that their influence will always be benign.

In sum, below-cost pricing combined with public and/or private subsidy creates a situation in which the integrity of the educational institution is not protected by that diffusion of economic power ranged against it which is the real protection of all units—households and firms alike—in a competitive market economy.

Note: The private colleges and universities—both because they depend more heavily on student fees and because they draw subsidies from a greater variety of sources—do seem more capable of maintaining an educationally efficient program than do the large, state-supported institutions. The argument is not that the public donor is more given to intervening or less tolerant than the private donor. The argument is that the public donor agency may have control of as much as 80 percent of the revenue sources of the institutions with which it is involved, whereas the private donor rarely has control over more than a small fraction of the revenue sources of the institutions with which he is involved.

Customer Control

But would not freeing the colleges from subsidy-oriented control and placing them under customer control be a move from the frying-pan into the fire? Is the college student really equipped to evaluate the service he is buying?[5]

This is a difficult question to answer. If I may be permitted to draw from my own experience as a college teacher and college dean, I would say that the student

[5] Thus, Howard Mumford Jones of Harvard University writes, "It is a misleading function when the concept of learning is, as is too often the case, sacrificed to the concept of teaching; when, for example, adolescents are solemnly asked to rate mature scholars in terms of their entertainment value in the classroom, and an administration in turn seriously accepts these callow judgments as a factor in the keeping and promoting of scholars." Howard Mumford Jones, "The Service of the University," *ACLS Newsletter,* Winter 1956–57, p. 12.

is a much better judge of the quality of the educational services he is receiving than he is commonly held to be. In the main, students *are* able to distinguish between those faculty members who provide excellent learning opportunities and those who provide mediocre or worse learning opportunities. The testimony on which the student has been convicted as a poor judge is the testimony of those who are themselves the object of the judging and who have traditionally resented the very practice of student appraisal.

And here again it must be remembered that the student's family often participates in the decision-making, adding the maturity of adult critical faculties to the immediate impressions of the student.

However, the greatest benefit to be derived from customer control is that the judgment of no one customer is critical to the operation of the institution. No small group of legislators, no small groups of corporations or individuals must be placated for the institution to survive and prosper. Nor need all institutions serve the same type of customer. The critical customer can be told to go elsewhere, because no one customer is of great significance. To repeat, it is not the restraint of the power wielders but the diffusion of power under customer control that protects the integrity of the institution.

In sum, below-cost pricing inevitably creates a threat to what has been called "academic freedom" (but what might better be called "educational efficiency"). To expect those who provide the subsidies to refrain from interfering with the operation of the school is to lean upon a demonstrably weak reed. On the other hand, to do as many feel appropriate, to somehow force the donors (perhaps through the operation of an organization like the American Association of University Professors) to keep their hands off the institutions they have subsidized is to deny another important freedom—the freedom of each man to choose the purposes to which his money resources are to be put. This is particularly true when the donor is the taxpayer who does not have the immediate option of stopping his contributions. He is ordered to pay and then is told that he must not question the purposes to which his funds are to be put. Under the system of below-cost pricing, there is no way of guaranteeing so-called "academic freedom" that does not involve a denial of other freedoms—or that does not demand of the donor a superhuman restraint from directing the uses to which his funds are to be allocated.

The Arguments for Below-Cost Pricing

Two primary arguments are advanced in support of below-cost pricing. One is based upon the assumption that the benefits of higher education flow not only to the students who are the direct customers of the schools, but also to society at large—that every member of society profits from being surrounded by and led by an educated citizenry. The other is the pure egalitarian argument that the principle of equality of opportunity demands that each young man and each young woman be given the opportunity of attending college, regardless of ability to pay for the services rendered. These arguments will be examined in turn.

The Social Benefits of Higher Education

The traditional thesis is that the student captures only a part of the gain that flows from his college education. Some part of the gain flows to society at large. Thus in the Northwest Ordinance of 1787 we find the following statement: "Religion, morality and knowledge being necessary to good government and the happiness of mankind, schools and the means of education shall forever be encouraged."

The student tends to push his purchases of education only to the point where the *private* gain from another unit would be equal to the cost of another unit. However, it is in society's interest that he push his purchases beyond this to the point where the *social* gain from another unit would be equal to the cost of that unit. This requires that the student receive a subsidy sufficient to induce him to purchase the additional units of education.

But even if this principle be accepted, below-cost

pricing does not inevitably follow. The subsidy could be provided directly to the student to permit him to pay the market price to whatever institution he chooses to attend. We have implemented our desire to provide bread to those who do not have the means to buy it, not by asking bakeries to sell all bread at below-market prices and then subsidizing the bakeries, but rather by providing a direct subsidy to the families involved. In particular, we have not insisted on the government actually operating bakeries to take care of this problem. The thesis under study does *not* establish a need for government-operated educational institutions, and in fact, on other grounds, there is good reason to prefer privately operated to publicly operated colleges and universities.

Nor does this thesis establish any case for below-cost pricing (or even for subsidy) of *all* the services now provided by higher education. It seems to establish a case only for those programs of education which contribute to the citizenship qualities of the individual. Surely those courses which are primarily *vocational* in nature make only an insignificant contribution to the development of the citizen.

Professor George Stigler of Columbia University has commented on this issue as follows:

> The basic defense for public and private subsidy of higher education is of course that it confers large social benefits, quite aside from any benefits accruing to the individual. This defense is largely wrong, simply as a matter

of fact. The majority of college students concentrate their efforts on vocational studies whose general social value is measured, comprehensibly and with tolerable accuracy, by the earnings of the graduates. In 1954, of 187,500 bachelor's and first professional degrees received by men in the United States, 63.1 percent were vocational degrees. For women the corresponding percentage was 54.8. The largest fields were:

Business Administration	35,255
Engineering	22,264
Education	16,885
Medical	16,458
Law	8,976
Agriculture	7,687

The general scientific and cultural values of these disciplines scarcely call for something like a 50 percent subsidy of the costs of institutions of higher learning.[6]

In sum, the principle of social benefit at best calls for subsidy only to the traditional liberal arts programs of colleges and universities and even there does not require below-cost pricing as the technique of implementation. Direct subsidy to the individual student would serve equally as well.

Finally, it might be argued that the social benefits deriving from formal higher education have been much exaggerated. These benefits probably come primarily at the lower levels of education, particularly in the in-

[6] George Stigler, "The Economic Theory of Education," unpublished manuscript.

struction each child receives in the basic skills of communication. Once a young person has acquired these skills, a whole world of knowledge is opened to him, a world in which formal classroom education is only one of the many alternatives. It would be difficult to prove that the college graduates in this country have been better citizens (even if a measure could be found) than the high school graduates. Far from underemphasizing the importance of higher education, we may have grossly exaggerated its importance to the maintenance of our free society.

The Egalitarian Argument

The second argument advanced in support of below-cost pricing is that equality of opportunity must be assured and that this demands equal educational opportunity for all.

In the first place, it should be pointed out that this too would justify only subsidy *in some form,* and provides no specific support for below-cost pricing of the services of higher education. On the contrary, below-cost pricing is a technique that subsidizes the sons and daughters of the wealthy as well as the sons and daughters of the poor. If the goal is to make education available to those who cannot afford it, below-cost pricing is a very blunt and wasteful instrument.

Thus, even if the egalitarian view is accepted, far

from justifying below-cost pricing, it condemns it as an inefficient means of achieving the desired end.

Education and Equality of Opportunity

But the thesis that equal access to higher education, regardless of financial ability to pay for it, is a *sine qua non* of equality of opportunity is not of unquestionable validity. Support for this thesis usually involves pointing to the demonstrably higher lifetime earnings of college graduates *vis à vis* nongraduates. The inference is drawn that the college education is itself the *cause* of the higher earnings.

One of the most important principles of statistics is that correlation is not the equivalent of causation. In this case, the high correlation between years of education and lifetime earnings may derive in part from the fact that those who attend college possess a generally higher potential to achieve than those who do not attend college. Thus, these same people would attain higher-income positions even if they were not to go to college. In the same way, those who attend college tend to come from higher-income families than those who do not attend college. Thus, they have such advantages as may come from a firmer financial base as a platform for the launching of a career. Finally, there is good evidence in the recent economic history of this country that a young man or woman without a college education is capable of making rapid economic progress.[7]

Moreover, those who wish to be educated do not face just the one alternative of formal, classroom education. Each person in our modern society is surrounded by opportunities for acquiring the knowledge, skills, and understandings that are the end-product of higher education. (One increasingly important set of such opportunities is to be found in the education programs sponsored by business firms for their employees. Moreover, there is evidence that the young adult, with some work experience behind him, makes better use of educational opportunities than does the young person of eighteen to twenty-two.)

In other words, there is no clear evidence that income-earning possibilities are a direct function of education. But even if this could be established, it would still be difficult to prove that formal college edu-

[7] One interesting reason for one advantage of the college graduate over the non-college person is to be found in the comment of an executive of one of the large steel companies. He says that his company hires so many college graduates each year in its executive development program, not because they have found college graduates to be clearly superior to non-graduates, but because the union rules on seniority prevent them from advancing the really good men from the work force into positions of responsibility. The same rules do not govern the young college graduates hired directly into the management group, and from this follows the company search for college graduates!

cation is the only kind of educational opportunity which promotes this end.

Admittedly, there are certain professions (e.g., law, medicine, and engineering) which are open only to those with a certain minimum of formal education. But in most of these cases, the lifetime earnings of those who received the training would easily permit them to pay for their education on a deferred-payment basis. All that is needed here is a capital market that will permit the treating of professional education as an investment in personal capital.

Confirmation of this thesis is found in one unexpected place: in a book whose central thesis is that higher education must be even more subsidized than at present, including a substantial increase in federal aid to higher education. The book is *A New Basis of Support for Higher Education*, and the author is Thad L. Hungate, Controller and Professor of Education, Teachers College, Columbia University.

In one paragraph he says, "While students and parents may continue to finance student living costs, neither fees nor living expenses should bar a student who has met defined state standards and has been admitted to and accredited for attendance. State aid should supplement family means as needed for this purpose." Yet in the very next paragraph he adds, "It is considered likely that each beneficiary of a college education so lifts his lifetime earnings that the increased taxes he pays will more than repay to society the initial capital it has invested in him."[8]

But if his increased earnings will permit him to repay the taxpayer, they will also permit him to repay a lending agency on the private capital market! Far from establishing a case for public subsidy, this statement weakens the case for public subsidy and strengthens the case for letting each student finance his own education from some combination of current and anticipated resources.

In sum, the argument that higher education must receive public subsidy to assure equality of income-earning possibilities is questionable in both theory and practice. There is no clear evidence that a formal, college education is itself a cause of higher lifetime earnings. But if it could be proven, it would establish not a need for public subsidy, but rather a need for an improved capital market to permit students to pay for their school out of the higher earnings produced by that schooling.

Conclusions

1. The present system of below-cost pricing of higher education creates a number of serious problems.

[8] Thad L. Hungate, *A New Basis of Support for Higher Education* (New York: Bureau of Publications, Teachers College, Columbia University, 1957), p. 7.

These include the problem of deciding which young people are to be admitted to college and then which are to be permitted to continue; the problem of low motivation of many students; the problem of motivation of faculty members created by the fact that they are not paid by their students; and the problem of educational efficiency created by the need to find resources to cover the annual deficits of colleges and universities.

2. The arguments presented to establish the desirability of public and/or private subsidy to higher education, even if accepted, do not demand below-cost pricing. They call only for subsidy in some form, and the problems associated with below-cost pricing suggest that the subsidy should be provided in other ways, perhaps through grants to individual students.

3. The arguments for subsidy to higher education are not of unquestionable validity. The "social benefit" argument seems to have been exaggerated and at best would apply only to the nonvocational types of higher education. The "equality of opportunity," in the opportunity-to-income sense, cannot be verified by a study of the recent economic history of this country. If it could be verified, it would establish not a case for subsidizing higher education, but rather a case for an improved capital market to permit students to borrow against future earnings to meet current educational expenses.

Recommendations

If the arguments developed in this paper were to be accepted as valid, what policy changes would seem to be required? Would these changes not call for an unrealistic assumption of the willingness on the part of the American people to modify the traditional arrangements in higher education?

Certainly, it is true that traditional arrangements cannot be changed quickly or with ease—and this is not an unmixed evil. A certain caution in making changes is usually wise.

It is particularly difficult to secure any reduction of subsidies to special groups, and in particular to secure reduction of subsidies coming from public funds. Those who lose the subsidy lose a considerable sum per capita; those who are relieved of paying for the subsidy gain only a small sum per capita. Thus, the subsidized tend to be much more vocal and aggressive than the subsidizers.

However, there is a growing awareness of the frightening financial load of higher education to be expected in the next ten or fifteen years. Some state legislators are already demanding that the state-supported schools increase tuition charges to students.

Clearly, any changes would have to begin with the charges of state-supported schools. *The private colleges and universities cannot hope to move closer to full-cost tuition charges until the tuition charges at state-*

supported schools are increased substantially. The differential in tuition costs already operates to place the private schools at a serious competitive disadvantage.

The first step would seem to be for state-supported institutions to set up a pattern of tuition increases designed to increase the percentage of costs covered by tuition payments. This pattern could call for a final position in which the revenues from tuition fees would be approximately equal to total costs. This could probably be done only if the state were to also provide an increasing supply of straight grants or loans to students. It would seem to be desirable to move as quickly as possible to the use of loans only to students pursuing strictly vocational courses, and to increase the ratio of loan money to grant money for all students. These loans and grants could also go to students attending privately operated colleges and universities. This would certainly be consistent with the general principle, but the private colleges would probably be able to bring students in touch with private sources of loan or scholarship money and would probably prefer to do so. In fact, there would be good reasons for the state governments to vacate the lending position as rapidly as the private money market could service the needs of students.

This paper is basically neutral on the question of whether government aid should come from local and state units or from the federal government. However, the principle of diffusion of power would seem to establish a preference for local and state units. Also, the general reduction in the financial responsibilities of government for higher education under this plan would largely dissipate the case now being made for federal aid to higher education.

It is probably unrealistic to expect that higher education in this country could be recast in the ultimate pattern implied in this study. But it is not unrealistic to suppose that progress could be made in bringing all tuition charges closer to the level of full cost, in greater use of loan techniques in the financing of all education and vocational education in particular, and in making greater use of the private capital market in the financing of investments in education. These changes would also tend to place an increasing emphasis on private as compared to public sponsorship of institutions of higher education.

If the arguments advanced in this paper are valid, all of these changes would work to the benefit of higher education and of the American society.

Chapter 2

The Promise of the College

There is one topic to which I can address myself that should be relevant to your lives and about which I have a very modest amount of specialized, personal knowledge. Most (perhaps all) of you are going on to college. What can you reasonably expect from your college experience? It is to this question that I intend to speak.

Let me put it another way: Led on in part by the promises made the colleges (as they have sought to lure you to their campuses), you must now have various expectations of the experiences ahead of you. Which of these expectations have some chance of being realized? Which of the promises of the college is it realistic to expect it to keep?

As my friend and colleague, George Stigler, professor of economics at the University of Chicago and long-time trustee of Carleton College, once put it: "The typical college catalogue would never stop Diogenes in his search for an honest man."

It is with no great pride and with an eye cocked for Ralph Nader that I confess to you that colleges promise prospective students (and their parents) many things, some of them obviously absurd, some of them partly attainable, some of them almost wholly attainable. Let's try to sort them out.

I'll begin with an easy one. Come to College A and life will be a ball and a ring-a-ding-ding, four years of fun and frolic. In the first place, if it really can deliver on this promise, College A isn't a college at all, but a kind of winter camp for aging teenagers. In the second place, the years from seventeen to twenty-two are destined by the nature of the human animal to be marked by fits of anxiety and concern, and by some very painful experiences.

Most of the problems will be highly personal and of a nature such that the college can be of almost no help. The love-hate relationship of the late-teens teenager and his or her parents; the sometimes embarrassing, but inevitable ending of old friendship patterns (including many that tonight you swear are fixed forever); and of course the now suddenly *serious* set of questions and dilemmas that arise out of the fact that there are two sexes and that it takes two to tango. Rare indeed is the mature person who, if given an opportunity, would set the time-machine back to these years of his or her life.

Let me hasten to add that not all need be painful or anxiety-creating or dull. These next few years for you will also include some wonderful and exciting experiences that you will indeed remember for the rest of your lives—not necessarily as they actually happened but as they are reconstructed at reunion time under the influence of Old Siwash and Old Crow. As a matter of fact, one of the most important reasons for going to college is that it *is* one of the most pleasant ways to spend these particular years in a person's life. In my opinion, "going to college" is in one sense largely a consumer good; an important part of the benefit flowing from it comes to end on the day you receive the degree. (All of us who make our lives and livings on campuses recognize this fact, but to many it is embarrassing to admit that they are engaged in serving such frivolous purposes as friendship, excitement, sentiment, and love. For myself, I see nothing wrong in so serving.)

My point is not that your college days will be, on balance, painful or pleasant, but only that the college itself, i.e., administration and faculty, will have little to do with it—except perhaps as it influences the quality of the other young people around you.

Let's turn to another one. Come to College B; our exciting new curriculum will guarantee you a superior education. Rogge's rule is that the more a college talks about its "exciting new curriculum," the less it really has to offer. Bring together competent, interesting faculty members and reasonably bright, interesting young people and something fine educationally is going to happen, regardless of the curriculum. Absent these two elements and nothing much is going to happen, however exciting the curriculum may appear to be. That doesn't mean that if you were to come to Wabash you wouldn't find us (even Ben Rogge) engaged in heated controversy over the Wabash curriculum. What you must understand is that struggles over the curriculum are to the faculty what intramural athletics are to the student body.

Here's another one: Come to College C and we'll prepare you for citizenship in the challenging, complex world of tomorrow. Who knows, perhaps the best way College C could deliver on this promise would be to teach you how to live off the land following an atomic disaster. Ah! you say, but perhaps College C can equip me to help save the world from an atomic disaster. Don't be too certain of that. The two countries most likely to launch an atomic disaster (one being our own) pride themselves on the literacy of their citizens and on the excellence of their programs of higher education. The system of higher education in Germany was the wonder of the world, copied in one country after another (including this country), and its scientists designed, among other things, the ingenious gas chambers at Dachau and Auschwitz.

I am not saying that education and good citizenship are inversely related. I am saying only that a strong, positive, and direct relationship has yet to be established. It may well be that the citizen whose education has come more from experience and from deep commitment to values than from the brittle world of on-campus intellectuality may be just as good a citizen as any of us with our college degrees. At the very least, this promise from College C can be no more than the expression of a pious wish until more evidence can be collected.

Here's one of the practical kind. Come to College D and you will certainly make more money in your adult years. Now, one piece of practical wisdom you may pick up in college is that correlation does not prove causation. Those who go to college do make more money than those who don't, but was it the going to college that *caused* the higher income?

The kind of person who has the brains, the drive, and, yes, the financial backing to go on to college would undoubtedly have made more money than others even if he or she hadn't gone to college. Some professions and some activities are open only to college graduates, but fortunately many avenues to high-income suburbs are open to all comers. As a matter of fact, there may well be a surplus of college-trained men and women; i.e., they may even now be more persons seeking the kind of employment and income associated with degree-holding than there are positions of this kind available. If your only interest is in making more money, don't go to college—become an apprentice plumber or beautician. In any case, the purposes of a true education have nothing to do with the making of money, except as an incidental and far from certain byproduct.

I suppose I should now stop shillyshallying and tell you what I, Ben Rogge, believe it *does* mean to be truly educated, to tell you what promise, if any, a college of integrity can reasonably make to prospective students, with some hope of delivering it. Here it is: a good college can say this: "We stand ready to confront you with a good faculty and a good group of fellow students. If you work at it (*an important if*) you will leave this place knowing more than when you entered it." That's it; that's all there is. Or I can put it this way, you will have all the personal advantages of knowing over not knowing. Moreover, you will know how to go about knowing even more for the rest of your life; you may even know what it is that is worth knowing and what it is that isn't worth knowing.

Hopefully, you will as well come to know how little you know, in fact how little is known about man and his world by even the most knowledgeable around you. This is to say that you may come to carry with you through life a deep sense of wonder and of awe, not of what you do understand, but of the deep and mysterious processes which neither you nor anyone else fully understands.

A brief interjection here: One of the ways in which

colleges (and college faculties in particular) have become corrupt in recent years has been the way in which they have sought to woo their students to their personal causes by assuring the students that they, the young, are possessed of a mystical wisdom, a godlike, compassionate understanding of life denied to all over age twenty-two, except of course those few adults who share the vision. This I believe to be nonsense.

Young people, and I mean you, *are* capable of being intelligent, courageous, selfless, and dedicated, but are *not* usually marked by the qualities of wisdom, tolerance, kindness and true compassion. I cannot urge you too strongly to beware of all adults who flatter you and tell you of your wisdom: we seek but to enlist you in our causes, whether of the left or the right or the middle, and we do not honestly believe you to be wise—nor are you, as a matter of fact.

To know more, yet to know how little you know—is that all there is to it?

Yes, that's about it. To know more may not be much and it may not be directly useful in the way the world measures usefulness, but at least it's something. To know more is at least to live an examined rather than an unexamined life; to live in an examined world rather than an unexamined world. In a world in which most human beings are said to live lives of quiet desperation, surely there is something to be said for this increased awareness, this increased perception of shades of meaning, of shades of beauty and ugliness and dissonance, of shades of dignity and integrity and vulgarity and hypocrisy.

Nor is respect for style an unimportant byproduct of knowing more. This sense for style, for *how* things are said or done, is often thought to be peripheral to the gutty business of life—or even of education. In fact, it seems to me to be one of those terribly important, self-imposed restraints which man has designed to keep himself from slipping back over the precipice into barbarism. Civilization is the most contrived, artificial, and delicate of man's creations, and its survival rests upon such slender reeds as man's cultivated sense of style—one of the byproducts of a true education.

With this education, this knowing more, should come as well a lifelong habit of observing all that happens, even what happens to you, with a certain detachment, a certain objectivity, a certain curiosity. In a sense, this may be a handicap to you, hold you back from passionate commitment to any single-track cause or single-minded interpretation of human experience—or if you do get so involved, you will occasionally be aware that what you are doing or saying may possibly be a trifle absurd.

What else? Let me conclude this somewhat rambling survey of the advantages of knowing more over knowing less with one more comment. Hopefully, the college that keeps this one meaningful promise will also have helped you, in the process, to become very careful about words. Words are the raw material of knowledge and in fact, of much of life, and they deserve to be treated with respect. The educated man or woman will always attempt to use them carefully and precisely and to demand of those who would communicate with him that they do the same. He will have learned that words can be used to inform or to deceive or to inspire or to confuse or to manipulate or to set into action—and will examine each important word used by another with the care and the suspicion with which an oriental peasant examines the fruit in a street market. When he finds a false one, he will reject it as convincingly as one of my favorite heroines of modern literature—and with this I reach the end.

This favorite heroine of mine is a little girl in an old cartoon in the *New Yorker* magazine. She is being force-fed by her mother, but is obviously rejecting whatever it is that is being offered her. Finally, in desperation, her mother says to her, "But dear, it's broccoli." At this, the little three-year-old girl in her high chair looks her mother in the eye and replies, "I say it's spinach and I say the hell with it!"

May the next four years be exciting and productive for you, and as you go on through life, may you gradually come to the knowledge of the difference between broccoli and spinach, and may you acquire the courage to challenge those who confuse the two.

Part IX

On What to Do

If you have stuck with me up to this point, you may be weary of one paragraph of despair after another, of one diagnosis after another of the ailments of present-day capitalism. If you share, in whole or in part, my conviction that capitalism is the only economic system consistent with the civilized life, you are probably anxious to move on from diagnosis to therapy. "What can I, as one person or as part of an organization, do about it? What would you have us do?"

As I say in the first paper of this section, "Frankly, I feel more at ease as the diagnostician than as the therapist." At the same time, I have discussed the question of what to do on various occasions, and three such discussion papers are presented here. The first paper was presented as an explicit follow-up to the Schumpeter-based "Can Capitalism Survive?" Various groups who were exposed to Schumpeter's analysis of things to come insisted that I come back with a message on how to keep those things from coming to pass. In Marxian language, in this paper I am trying to tell the bourgeoisie how to avoid being expropriated.

The second paper was written approximately a month before the presidential election of 1964. It is now clear that, at that time, I overestimated the damage that would be done to the conservative cause by a crushing defeat of Goldwater. At the same time, the course of events seems to me to have left my general conclusions on what to do largely untouched.

The final paper was given as a tribute to one man and the organization he created—to Leonard Read and the Foundation for Economic Education. It is with pleasure that I make public payment of my great debt to this man, but the paper is presented here because in writing it I found some ways of saying certain things on the practice of freedom that I have not been able to improve upon elsewhere.

Chapter 1

The Businessman and the Defense of Capitalism

The question before this house is not whether the survival of capitalism is in doubt (this is admitted). The question for us, as it was for Lenin at an earlier time, is, What to do? His concern was how best to hasten the collapse of capitalism; our concern is how to postpone or ward off that collapse.

Frankly, I feel more at ease as the diagnostician than as the therapist. Cancer is still easier to identify than to cure and so is overexpanded government. Admittedly, diagnosis must usually precede therapy. After a lengthy diagnostic examination, the doctor looks up at the patient in some puzzlement and asks, "Have you had this before?" To this the patient replies, "Yes," and the doctor says, "Well, you've got it again." Quite obviously something more than this is needed. Proper therapy usually rests upon diagnosis of the specific problem, including some notion of how the patient got into his fix, whatever it might be.

I begin then with the question, "What is our problem?" In an earlier sentence, I identified the problem as that of overexpanded government. This is not really correct for the purposes of therapy. Overexpanded government is, in fact, but the most noticeable, objectively evident *symptom* of our problem. Our problem is in the form of a set of ideas whose implementation calls for the use of force, and government is that agency of society given a monopoly of the right to use force. For so long as those ideas are dominant in society, Behemoth will continue to grow. Nor is it useful for those who hold and espouse those ideas publicly to regret the associated growth in government and all its instrumentalities. Thus Senator Edward Kennedy has said recently that "one of the greatest dangers of government is bureaucracy," and Senator Gaylord Nelson has said, "The federal bureaucracy is just an impossible monstrosity." All well and good, but that growth in bureaucracy which they so rightly lament is the necessary and inevitable outcome of the ideas that these two (and others) have so well and so convincingly espoused.

What are these ideas that produce bureaus as larvae do moths? They can be expressed in various ways but their essence is to be found in the following related propositions:

(1) There exist individuals and groups in society who know not only what is best for them but what is best for others as well.

(2) This wisdom, when combined with the coercive power of the state, can be used to produce "the good society." An accurate verbalization of these ideas is to be found in the statement of Newton Minnow, who said as chairman of the agency controlling television in this country, "What is wrong with the television industry in this country is that it is giving the viewers what they (the viewers) want."

Compare this, for example, with these words from Adam Smith's *Wealth of Nations:*

> What is the species of domestic industry which his capital can employ, and of which the produce is likely to be of the greatest value, every individual, it is evident, can, in his local situation, judge much better than any statesman or lawgiver can do for him. The statesman, who should attempt to direct private people in what manner they ought to employ their capitals, would not only load himself with a most unnecessary attention, but assume an authority which could safely be trusted, not only to no single person, but to no council or senate whatever, and which would nowhere be so dangerous as in the hands of a man who had folly and presumption enough to fancy himself fit to exercise it.[1]

Some of you may see in other idea-systems (such as economic determinism, relativism, envy, or what have you) the real source of our malignancy. God, my wife, my children, and all of you know that I am fallible,

---

[1] Adam Smith, *The Wealth of Nations* (New York: Modern Library, 1937), p. 423.

and perhaps I have chosen poorly in this case. What I *am* prepared to argue in a more strenuous way is my conviction that our struggle is at the level of ideas and not that of men or institutions. In the words of the celebrated John Maynard Keynes,

> The ideas of economists and political philosophers both *when they are right and when they are wrong,* are more powerful than is generally understood. Indeed, the world is ruled by little else. Practical men, who believe themselves to be quite exempt from any intellectual influences, are usually the slaves of some defunct economist. Madmen in authority, who hear voices in the air, are distilling their frenzy from some academic scribbler of a few years back.[2]

My first point then is that we are involved in a war of ideas. My second is that our target is not the masses but those men and women in society who deal in ideas and who shape the thinking of the masses. In the words of one of the great idea men of this century, the late Ludwig von Mises, "The masses, the hosts of common men, do not conceive any ideas, sound or unsound. They only choose between the ideologies developed by the intellectual leaders of mankind. But their choice is final and determines the course of events. If they prefer bad doctrines, nothing can prevent disaster."[3]

[2] John Maynard Keynes, *The General Theory of Employment, Interest, and Money* (New York: Harcourt Brace, 1936), p. 383.

[3] Ludwig von Mises, *Human Action* (Chicago: Henry Regnery Co., 1963), p. 864.

My third point is that the ideas that finally count are those that relate to such fundamental questions as the nature of man, his purpose here on earth, and the moral character of human action. Arguments on the basis of economic efficiency are not alone capable of saving capitalism.

In the words of Joseph Schumpeter: "It is an error to believe that political attack (of capitalism) arises primarily from grievance and that it can be turned by justification. Political criticism cannot be met by rational argument. Utilitarian reason is in any case weak as a prime move of group action. In no case is it a match for the extra-rational determinants of conduct. The stock exchange is a poor substitute for the Holy Grail."[4]

I have now enumerated my assumptions as to the nature of the task in which we are involved. I have argued that we are really involved in a struggle for the souls of men, that in that struggle it is ideas that count, and that the questions that are relevant are largely ethical in nature. Moreover, I have argued that our target is not the masses but those who live by the spoken and written word and who thus largely shape opinion in society.

If these assumptions be even roughly valid, what then is implied as to the role of the businessman in

---

[4] Joseph A. Schumpeter, *Capitalism, Socialism, and Democracy,* 3rd ed. (New York: Harper & Row, 1962), pp. 144, 137.

the fight to save capitalism? Before attempting an answer to that question, let me consider one that seems to precede it. Should the businessman *as businessman* even get involved in the struggle?

A number of factors would seem to indicate a negative answer to that question. To begin with, the businessman is not typically hired by the stockholders to carry on programs of social reforms; he is hired to add to the net worth of the company. Admittedly the net worth of the company may be adversely affected by particular acts of government, and the stockholders would surely approve of management action in opposition to those specific threats to profits—for so long as the potential gain exceeded the cost. At the same time, the company may often stand to gain through specific acts of government, including actions that work *against* the principles of capitalism. Is it a tariff against foreign steel producers? or an export subsidy that would increase the demand for the company's products? or a government-enforced price or interest rate that adds to the profits of the company? How now the businessman? How can the president of the Mobil Oil Company be a convincing spokesman for free enterprise when his job seems to require that he oppose immediate decontrol of oil prices? How can the president of General Electric stand four-square for capitalism, yet support export subsidies for many of the products sold by his firm?

The fact is that there is hardly a businessman in this country who is not receiving favors from government in one way or another. The fact that this is true of most other elements in the society, including his critics in the ranks of the intellectuals, does not really change the nature of the businessman's dilemma. His job may seem to require of him that he support specific government intervention in the economy of precisely the kind that, in the fight for men's souls, he must condemn as general practice. Knowledge of Kant's Categorical Imperative—do only that which you would be willing to see done by all—may get you an A in a college course in philosophy but may get you fired if you attempt to practice it as a businessman.

In other words, his very position may seem to require of the businessman that, in the struggle against government intervention, he be as often a part of the problem as of the solution. Moreover, how can he face those he is attempting to persuade to hold the capitalist faith when his own hands are so obviously unclean?

A second reason for a possible negative answer to the question of whether the businessman should get into the fight to save capitalism is that he is usually an amateur in the practice of the arts required by that struggle. The art required is not that of making or selling men's suits or aircraft motors; the art is that of the dealer in abstract ideas, including and particularly systems of ethical judgment. Don't misunderstand me;

it is not that the businessman is unintelligent. I yield to no one in my respect for the great practical and theoretical intelligence required for effective entrepreneurship. It is simply that his intelligence is not applied, day in and day out, to the kinds of questions and considerations that are at the center of the argument. Not only is this not his turf, but he is usually not adept at the word games that go on on that turf.

What I am saying in essence is that here, as in most of life, the prizes (in this case, the souls of men) will go largely to those who are specialists in the arts involved. Admittedly there are some such (I could name you a dozen or so) from the ranks of the businessmen, but their skills in the arena of ideas and words are not a product of their business experience but of what they have done on their own initiative to improve their own understanding of the ideas involved here and their skills in communicating those ideas.

Where then does this leave us? Can the typical businessman do nothing but deplore the growth of government and go on about his task—which may have been made easier in some ways and more difficult in other ways by that self-same expansion of government involvement in economic life? I believe that the answer to that question is "no"—but I have some real sympathy with those businessmen (and this will be the great majority) who by their inaction say "yes." After all, as Henry David Thoreau put it, "I came into this world, not chiefly to make this a good place to live in, but to live in it, be it good or bad."[5] Nor, as I have argued elsewhere, is it the administrator-businessman who has the most to lose from the passing of capitalism. Most of them will end up as administrators of socialist enterprises if and when full socialism arrives. It is the masses who have the most to lose—and who also have the least understanding of that fact.

But for those of you who *are* interested in doing something as business and professional people to counter the drift to collectivism, here is what I would suggest that might be both useful *and* consistent with the profit-oriented role for which you draw your pay.

(1) Work with your own staff members and employees. A work force that has some understanding of the marketplace and of where its own goodies come from *may* (and it is only a *may*) be a less troublesome, more effective work force over time. Any number of such programs, of varying effectiveness, are now in operation and available for general use.

(2) Work with the appropriate audiences in the communities where you have operations. Here again, there may be some payoff in terms of a better political environment in which to function. Again, there are a number of such programs now in operation.

[5] Henry David Thoreau, "Civil Disobedience," in *Walden and Other Writings* (New York: Modern Library), p. 645.

Anything more? Frankly, I am not much impressed by the usefulness of business attempts to reach nationwide audiences with free-enterprise propaganda.

What else? The "else" is what the businessman *shouldn't do* rather than what he should do. Moreover, it requires that the individuals involved must have done their *own* homework.

In fact, let me say right now that even the first two steps I have identified can do more harm than good if the people selecting and authorizing the operations have not themselves taken the time and effort to decide exactly what it is they believe and why. There is nothing about being a successful businessman (even a *very* successful businessman) that automatically endows one with an understanding of or an attachment to the principles of freedom—a statement I could support with a hundred examples, if time permitted. In fact, some of the great fortunes of America have been made by those who have learned how to use government intervention to their own advantage.

I cannot emphasize too strongly that the very first thing each of you who wishes to be a truly effective part of this struggle must do is your own homework. This requires reading, thinking and, yes, writing. I challenge each of you to go home tonight and put down in brief form your guiding principles in life and their applications in this area of the relationship of the individual to his government. You might also find it interesting to follow that with a list of those things which you and/

or your company or group are now doing that are clear or possible violations of those principles.

Am I asking you to immediately cease all ideological wrongdoing? to cut yourself off completely from all areas of government involvement? Were you to do so, there would be literally no way you could eat or move about or keep warm or survive—such is the extent of government's involvement in our lives. Each of you, in your professional role, must decide for yourself the limits of your compromise with the apparent demands of the moment.

Let me summarize:

(1) I am arguing that the first and indispensable step for any person who wishes to be a part of the effort to save capitalism is a determination of precisely what he believes and why. This will usually involve, not just putting down the already determined, but active study, reflection, and discussion. This is your intellectual and philosophical armor, and without it you are not only vulnerable but as likely to be a handicap as a help in the struggle.

(2) Try as best you can in this imperfect world to live by those principles.

(3) In using your professional role or your company in the struggle, do only those things that seem consistent with the long-run interests of those whose

money you are using. Remember, not all stockholders will wish to have their money used in this or any other crusade.

(4) If you wish to play a personal role, apart from your company or professional connection, then you must dig deeper into what you believe and why; you must know even more fully the arguments and values of those with whom you disagree; you must continually seek to improve your skill in expressing your ideas and in demonstrating the errors in contrary positions. My guess is that only a few of you will carry through to this level of participation—but it is not a numbers game anyway; it is a game in which it is the quality of the few that finally counts.

I spoke earlier of the things that you should *not* do but didn't specify them. What are they?

(a) Don't make a pest of yourself by trying to force your free-enterprise ideas down the throat of every passerby—whether in your home, your office, or at the cocktail party. In the words of Leonard Read, founder and president of the Foundation for Economic Education, who has taught me everything I know on this and many other questions, "Go only where called—but do your damnedest to get good enough to be called."

(b) You may not be able to avoid involvement in departures from principle, but at least don't lend your voice or your money to the support of those departures.

You may have to pay into social security or submit to a system of wage-price controls but you don't have to join committees or groups who support such programs.

In a hundred different ways and forms, the American businessman is aiding and abetting the enemy by continuing his involvement in organizations and programs which are as likely to propose as to oppose extensions of government. Don't let this reciprocity game you people of substance play with each other or your desire to be a good guy lead you to give your money and/or your name (and hence, by implication, your support) to activities or organizations that are working the other side of the freedom street.

To return to Thoreau:

> It is not a man's duty, as a matter of course, to devote himself to the eradication of any, even the most enormous wrong; he may still properly have other concerns to engage him; but it is his duty, at least, to wash his hands of it, and, if he gives it no longer thought, not to give it practically his support.[6]

Forgive me if I seem to blaspheme, but even your church and your college should be examined with some care before you bless them with your dollars and your support. You don't have to prove you are a nice, broad-minded guy by providing the devil with the coal for your own burning.

---

[6] Ibid., p. 642.

Again to be specific, you needn't insist that every professor on your old campus think exactly as you do, but I believe it completely appropriate for you to find out if the general idea system that *you* believe to be best is well and ably represented in the ranks of the faculty.

I close this sermon with these words: Avoid anger, recriminations, and personal attack. Those with whom you are angry are probably (taken by and large) at least as filled with or as empty of virtue as you. Moreover, they are the very ones you might wish later to welcome as your allies.

Avoid panic and despair; be of good cheer. If you're working in freedom's vineyard to the best of your ability, the rest is in the hands of a higher authority anyway. If you can see no humor in what's going on (and even at times in your own behavior) you'll soon lose that sense of balance so important to effective and reasoned thought and action.

Finally, take comfort in the thought that the cause of freedom can never be lost, precisely because it can never be won. Given man's nature, freedom will always be in jeopardy and the only question that need concern each of us is if and how well we took our stand in its defense during that short period of time when we were potentially a part of the struggle.

Chapter 2

Reflections on the Election of 1964

By the time this is in print, the election will be over and conservatism as a potent political force will be dead. A fine man will have suffered a humiliating defeat, and the liberals in his party will be planning a ruthless purge of all those who were closely associated with his candidacy. The stage will have been set for the specter of the "Goldwater debacle" to haunt the candidacy of every conservative for years to come.

In the meantime, his most passionate supporters will be using their special journals of opinion to vent their disappointment and bitterness in angry explanations of why it happened. Some will say that the campaign was badly conducted (which it was); some, that Goldwater was sabotaged by the liberals of the press, radio, and television (which he was); some, that he was defeated by one of the most effective, ruthless, and corrupt politicians of the modern era (which may or may not be true). The Minutemen will be laying in more rifles and the president of the John Birch Society will be proving to his own satisfaction that Goldwater's defeat was engineered by members of his own party, acting as conscious agents of the Communist conspiracy.

The truth, I suspect, lies quite elsewhere, and it is that possibility I wish to explore. My own interpretation of the election can be simply stated: In a democratic society, under normal circumstances, no radical reorientation of social policy can be achieved by simple political organization and political action. Or to put it another way: As a general rule, for groups concerned with ultimate principles, elections just don't matter!

Let me put it still another way: Given the absence of any feeling of crisis in the American society and given the general acceptance of modern liberalism by most Americans who count, Goldwater was foredoomed to crushing defeat. All of this was perfectly evident long before Goldwater was nominated. The great mistake was made, not during the campaign, but precisely when those conservatives who pride themselves on being activists and on "knowing how to get things done" decided that conservatism could be brought to America by what would amount to a political *coup*. Goldwater's own clear, good sense in thinking that the time was not ripe and that he could serve the cause better by continuing as senator from Arizona was overpowered by the passion of the leaders of the Draft Goldwater group and by their assurance that they had the know-how to get the job done.[1]

This assurance was bolstered by the ease with which the organization swept through the San Francisco convention. But of course it is no great task for a well-organized minority to take over a committee (and that is what a political convention most resembles); in fact, it is done every day. It is a much more difficult task to get a man elected, particularly one for whose ideas the time is far from ripe.

Goldwater might have won, had the country been plunged in a deep crisis of some kind at the time of the campaign. The victories of the Erhard "social market economy" in Germany in the late forties and more recently of the conservatives in Brazil were both made possible by the widespread sense of impending disaster in the societies involved. As John Maynard Keynes wrote, with such excellent foresight, in 1936, "At the present moment people are unusually expectant of a more fundamental diagnosis; more particularly ready to receive it; eager to try it out, if it should be even plausible."[2] Certainly the philosophical and political success of the ideas he presented in the book in which

[1] See William A. Rusher, "Suite 3505: The Inside Story of How, When and Where the Goldwater Candidacy Was Conceived and Launched," *National Review,* August 11, 1964, pp. 683–86.

[2] J. M. Keynes, *The General Theory of Employment, Interest and Money* (New York: Harcourt, Brace, 1936), p. 383.

these words appear would attest to the significance of timing in attempts at radical change.

In any case, it was precisely those who pride themselves on their practical wisdom who launched this most impractical of all modern political actions. *The country was simply not yet prepared to accept the conservative position. Goldwater's campaign could not build on any solid foundation of widely accepted ideas on society, economics, and the state.*

This became apparent the moment Goldwater made the slightest threatening gesture in the direction of any specific element in the welfare state, e.g., social security. The response was so immediate and frightening that his campaign strategy made an obvious switch, to concentrate on corruption in the Johnson administration and to promise a rather mystical rebirth of honesty and integrity in government and of "morality" in society.

As Hayek pointed out to us long ago, honesty and integrity in government are not a function of which party is in power but of the power over economic decisions possessed by those in government.[3] But the people were not ready to reduce the power of government, and Goldwater and his advisors had no place else to go. The basic argument over principles had to be aban-

[3] F. A. Hayek, *The Road to Serfdom* (Chicago: University of Chicago Press, 1944), particularly the chapter on "Why the Worst Rise to the Top."

doned because most of the people weren't ready to accept the Goldwater principles. When the debate turned to who could do better what we're now doing, the man in the saddle in a period of relative prosperity had a crushing advantage.

Nor could much be made out of foreign policy issues. Goldwater's interventionist posture in foreign affairs was just like Johnson's, only more so. The Goldwater principles of nonintervention and limited government on the domestic scene mixed poorly with his promise of aggressive, interventionist action on the foreign scene. Whether he was more or less right than Johnson on foreign policy is not at issue. The question is whether there was any fundamental difference between the two in principle, and no such difference could be made to stick (not even the charge that Johnson was "soft on communism"). Again it became a question of who could better do what we are now doing, and again the man in the saddle had an overwhelming advantage.

Let me repeat: Goldwater lost because those who count in America weren't prepared to accept his ideas. The lesson would seem to be that *the real function of conservatism in America is not to try to win elections but to try to win converts.* The real battle is, as always, a battle of ideas.

Henry David Thoreau once wrote, "It matters less what name I drop into the ballot box on election day than what kind of man I drop from my chambers into the street each morning." I would paraphrase this to read, "It matters less what name I drop into the ballot box on election day than what ideas I drop into the common pool during my lifetime."

Not a single one of the principles of limited government and individual freedom has been proved wrong by the Goldwater defeat (just as not a single one would have been proved right by a Goldwater victory). Not a single principle of the interventionist, welfare state has been proved right by the Johnson victory.

Ideas are still evaluated by a different and more fundamental process, and perhaps it is time that we got back to work on that process. Let us forget for awhile all attempts to be clever at political organization. Let us return to our problems of understanding, analysis, and clarity of exposition of the ideas of freedom. If we do our work well, we may some day be rewarded by the only lasting kind of political victory—a situation in which the ideas of freedom are so generally accepted in *both* parties that it will make little difference which one wins.

Chapter 3

The Foundation for Economic Education: Success or Failure?

The question before us is this: Has the Foundation for Economic Education, in its first twenty-five years, succeeded in its mission? Most speakers on such occasions are capable of supplying only one answer to such a question. Tonight, at no extra cost to you, I intend to give you *four* answers to this question. They are in order: yes, probably no, almost certainly no, and unqualifiedly yes. Are there any questions?

The reason I can give you four answers to this one question is that the phrase, "succeeded in its mission," is capable of at least four meaningful interpretations, each calling for its own answer.

One possible interpretation is that the mission of any organization, at first instance, is quite simply to survive. That FEE has survived is testified to by our presence here tonight. Nor should any of us think lightly of this accomplishment. Given the general social and economic climate of the immediate postwar period, the survival chances of any organization committed to individual freedom and limited government could well have been described in 1946 as two in number: slim and none.

So much, you might think, for the criterion of mere survival—but survival is not as "mere" as you might think. Never underestimate the significance of the simple fact of the continuing existence of an island of sanity in an increasingly insane world. Whether this sanity can eventually turn the battle is still moot and will be discussed in a moment, but its simple existence is a very present help in time of trouble.

I am reminded of Tolstoy's description of the role of the Russian commander, Prince Bagration, in the battle of Schön Grabern. Although himself in doubt of the outcome and aware of how little he really knew of the battle's progress, the Prince stood serene and confident in the view of all, answering each report of the action, whether encouraging or discouraging, with a sonorous, "Very good!"—as if even the local defeats were part of an overall pattern of events that foretold ultimate victory. As Tolstoy put it:

> Prince Andrew noticed that . . . though what happened was due to chance and was independent of the commander's will, his (Bagration's) presence was very valuable. Officers who approached him with disturbed countenances became calm; soldiers and officers greeted him gaily, grew more cheerful in his presence, and were evidently anxious to display their courage before him.[1]

[1] Tolstoy, *War and Peace,* Inner Sanctum ed., p. 193.

As with these soldiers, we grow more cheerful in the presence of FEE and Leonard Read, more anxious to display our limited courage. Believe me, this is something; even though the battle itself were to be already lost, as it well may be, FEE, as the island of sanity to which we repair for warmth and comfort, may still be counted a great and significant success.

A second way to evaluate an organization is to examine its chances for survival in the long run. Do we have here an organization so significant and successful that it will live through the centuries (or at least the decades) ahead?

Not only do I answer, "Probably no," to this question but I add "and I hope not" to that answer. The real danger to an organization of this kind is not that it will simply disappear, but that its *form* will long survive its *soul.*

Do not misunderstand me; I am not forecasting an early end to FEE. It is true that even Leonard Read is not immortal, but Read's leaving will not mean the end of this organization. It will carry on, and for *x* number of years, continue to be a center of strength in the cause of freedom.

But times change, and people change, and institutions change; it is as certain as death itself that sooner or later FEE will be, in spirit, something quite different from what it now is. Moreover, the chances are that that spirit will be significantly alien to the spirit that now moves this organization.

When that day comes, if any of us are still around,

let us have the courage and good sense to give FEE a decent burial, rather than yield to a pagan attachment to a body from which the spirit has already fled. The world of organizations is cluttered with deformed and defaming relics of noble causes; let FEE not be one of them.

We turn now to a third possible interpretation of success as it relates to the work of FEE. Has FEE succeeded in its mission in the sense of being a part of an action that promises to actually turn the tide of battle in the direction of freedom? My answer to this is, "almost certainly no."

I offer this not as a criticism of the work of FEE but as what seems to me to be the only realistic appraisal of where the current of events is tending in this world. The situation in this world, as it relates to individual freedom, is almost certain to become much worse, before *and* if it ever becomes any better. Why must I adopt this apparently defeatist line and on this should-be gladsome occasion in particular?

My own none-too-original analysis of the trend of events tends to bring me into agreement with the many friends and foes of capitalism alike who believe that the odds are very much against the survival of capitalism in the decades immediately ahead of us.

This is not the time or the place for a detailed presentation of the analysis that leads me to this conclusion. Moreover, my thesis has been more cogently reasoned and more ably presented in the works of Schumpeter, Mises, Hayek, Popper, and others.

I offer only the following straws in the wind. First, there is the incredible recrudescence of the most primitive forms of utopianism. Young people (and old) possessed of superior intellectual equipment (as measured by aptitude tests) are every day repeating to me, in one form or another, the chiliastic musings of Marx in his *German Ideology:*

> In communist society, where nobody has an exclusive sphere of activity but each can become accomplished in any branch he wishes, society regulates the general production and thus makes it possible for me to do one thing today and another tomorrow, to hunt in the morning, fish in the afternoon, rear cattle in the evening, criticize after dinner, just as I have a mind.

I am not surprised to find that the young are enchanted by visions of a do-your-own thing New Jerusalem, complete with almost continuous love-play; after all, even the brightest of the young tend to think largely with the heart and the loins. What shocks me is that supposedly mature scholars either encourage them in their daydreaming or hesitate to bring their schemes to full and vigorous and rational challenge.

Nowhere is this denial of reason, of process, of rational choice more clearly revealed than in the approach of the more demented environmentalists. In one of the best critiques of this approach I know, an article in *The Public Interest,* the author writes as follows: "Those who call for immediate action and damn the cost, merely because the spiney starfish and furry crab populations are shrinking, are putting an infinite marginal value on these creatures. This strikes a disinterested observer as an overestimate."[2]

But the voice of reason is rarely raised and is shouted down by the new romantics (and the new barbarians) as soon as it is raised.

Lady Chatterley's lover, once a hero of the young and the teachers of English literature for his sexual acrobatics, is now their hero as the man who said, "It's a shame, what's been done to people these last hundred years: men turned into nothing but labor-insects, and all their manhood taken away. . . . I'd wipe the machines off the face of the earth again, and end the industrial epoch absolutely, like a black mistake."

It is symptomatic of the times that a call like this for over 90 percent of those now living in the Western world to be wiped out (for such would be the effect of such a proposal) is hailed as a voice of humanitarianism and love, while those who dare to offer even gentle caveats are derided as gross and disgusting materialists.

So much for the treason of the intellectuals, a treason that Mises and Hayek and Schumpeter forewarned us of, and one that is now largely a fact. If FEE is to be judged by its success in swinging the intellectual vote, then it has failed indeed.

What of the businessman? Surely FEE and its com-

---

[2] Larry Ruff, "The Economic Common Sense of Pollution," *The Public Interest,* Fall 1970, p. 74.

panion organizations have been able to make secure for freedom this section of the American public! At this point, it is difficult to know whether to laugh or cry. There is not one piece of lunacy put on paper by some academic scribbler or spoken by some public demagogue that is not to be found in at least one, if not more, of the published statements of the self-designated spokesmen for the business community. For reasons that I don't have time to develop here, it is also clear that the larger the firm, the more certain is its leaders' commitment or at least lip service to the philosophy of statism. Study the changing character of the business firms that have contributed to FEE over the last twenty-five years. In the first years, at least a dozen of the largest, best-known firms in this country were making direct contributions to FEE. Less than a handful are still on the list of donors. Those socialists and those defenders of capitalism who expect the average American businessman to put up a desperate fight in defense of the system are simply out of touch with the situation as it really is.

Yes, even the businessman is more likely to be a part of the problem than a part of the solution, and FEE's failure, so judged, could not be more obvious or complete. But of course, contrary to the popular impression, there is no reason to expect the businessman to be more committed to the system of economic freedom than anyone else. Not only is he *not* the greatest beneficiary of that system—he is not even the *principal* beneficiary. Again contrary to the popular impression, it is the "little man," the member of the masses who, far from being the exploited victim under capitalism, is precisely its principal beneficiary. Under all other arrangements, those possessed of intelligence, high energy, and a strong desire to achieve (i.e., precisely those who tend to become the entrepreneurs, the businessmen under capitalism) get ahead by using their positions in the political or caste or religious hierarchy to exploit the masses. Only under capitalism can the stronger get ahead only by serving the weaker—*and as the weaker wish to be served*! (Ralph Nader to the contrary.)

The strong tend to survive and prosper under any system, and strength does not necessarily carry with it a sophisticated understanding of systems. The American businessman has probably been, on balance (wittingly or unwittingly), the most important single force working against the capitalist system.

This brings us to another of the straws in the wind. If further evidence of where we seem to be headed is needed, I offer you the current [Nixon] administration in Washington, D.C. It is manned by a number of intelligent, capable public servants of roughly conservative outlook and headed by an intelligent, well-meaning man of sound conservative instincts [*sic*]. Yet I am prepared to wager that history will reveal that no administration in modern times did more to move the country away from freedom and toward socialism and authoritarianism than the one now in power. I say this in sorrow, not anger, sorrow at the fact that the prevailing ideology of the day traps even the apparent foes into serving its cause, once they acquire political power. If the prevailing climate is interventionist, a conservative administration will not only be compelled to serve that climate of opinion but will be able to command a larger consensus for interventionist actions than an openly left-wing administration could ever command. In addition, the man on the street (who, in my opinion, also has generally conservative instincts) is less on his guard when a group identified as conservative is in power—and is thus largely unaware as one socialist scheme after another is imposed upon him.

In other words, wherever we look—to the intellectuals, to the businessmen, to the political leaders—we find the score to be Lions, 100; Christians, Zero. If FEE's mission has been to win such games in the here and now, then it is indeed a one-hundred carat failure. Not only has FEE not turned the tide of battle, the situation in this country has gotten steadily worse in every one of the last twenty-five years and promises to get even worse in the next twenty-five.

Am I predicting that we are inevitably headed for a great, all-encompassing crisis at some time in the next few decades? I am not. In the first place, nothing is inevitable. What has happened has happened because of decisions made by human beings and could be undone by the decisions of human beings in the years ahead. I am simply saying that if things continue to go as they have been going (as seems likely), we are going to move further and further away from reasonable prosperity and substantial freedom, and toward stagnation and authoritarianism.

If any of you have seen FEE's mission as that of winning now and winning big, then you have no choice but to label it a failure. But as I have understood him, his thinking, and the organization he brought into being, I have always believed that Leonard Read saw his mission as something quite different from (and quite superior to) that of winning tomorrow's election or next week's idea popularity poll. He seems little interested in triumphs as spectacular and as short-lived as the hula hoop.

Again let us be honest with each other. I suspect (I know) that this aspect of FEE's thinking has been occasionally irritating to many of you and particularly to the more activist-minded of you. Read must have been about as satisfying to you at times as would be a football coach at your alma mater who asked for fifty years to do a rebuilding job with the team. Who knows, they might not even be reporting the scores to the local papers where Rogge and Read and many of you will be fifty years from now. You would like to see (and in person) the old scoreboard light up and read, Christians, 100; Lions, Zero. If that really is your goal, then you are at the wrong dinner for the wrong man.

Not only does Read not promise us a win in the *near*

future; not only does he not guarantee us a win in the *distant* future; he has the unmitigated gall to tell us that we still don't even fully understand the game or how to recognize a win when we see one. Finally, he refuses us even the consolation of the assurance that while *we* may not know the full truth, *he* does and will tell us all about it. Stop worrying about such things, he tells us; "the readiness is all." Here are some typical statements from this strange and difficult man:

> Not a man among us is entitled to look down his nose at any other; scarcely anyone has more than scratched the surface. And there are reasons aplenty: the complexities of this subject are akin to the mysteries of Creation.
>
> Always skeptical of activist efforts, I have, until this moment, agreed that our own work has only long-range prospects—preserving the remnant, as it were. Now I see it the other way around; the chance of getting results here and now lies exclusively in the study and exposition of ideas on liberty.
>
> The freedom idea is in fact a recent, idealistic, elevated acquisition of the human mind. Not being rooted in tradition and having little in the way of second-nature behaviors working for its security, it lacks stability; it is easily lost; freedom concepts are fragile, wonderful ideas, few of which we've yet embraced by second nature within our relatively unconditioned consciousness.
>
> Freedom will always be insecure; it will forever be touch-and-go. Even eternal vigilance and devoted effort can do no more than to set the trend aright, as high an aim as we should embrace. And this expectation is warranted only if we view our problem realistically, see it as profound

> and difficult as it really is. To assess it superficially, to think of it as requiring anything less than practices consonant with freedom becoming second nature, is to waste our time and energy, to spin our wheels, as the saying goes.
>
> Is this too dismal a prospect? Not to those among us who enjoy a challenge; it's magnificent!

How can he call magnificent a challenge where the odds-makers have installed the Lions as 100-point favorites? Because, he tells us, "it is the effort, not the outcome, that counts in the life of the human being." "Cervantes', 'The road is better than the inn,' should serve to remind aspiring men that there isn't any inn for them, but only the road, now and forever. It is the effort along the trail that matters."

And now the final interpretation of the phrase "succeeded in its mission": Leonard Read's *own* definition of how the success of a FEE (of a Leonard Read) should be measured:

"To measure a teacher's success, to evaluate his work, one must ask: Does the teaching induce in others what Aristotle termed 'activity of soul'?"

It is to this question that the final and unqualified and only significant "yes" can be given. Throughout this country, throughout the world there is "activity of soul" underway that would never have been undertaken but for the work and the inspiration of Leonard Read and the Foundation for Economic Education. Some of it all of us in this room know about and can identify with FEE; some of it is known to only one or two of those in this room; the greater part, and probably the most important part, is totally unknown as yet to any of us (including Leonard Read) and will come to light only in the decades and centuries ahead—and much of it will be done by people who will never have heard of this foundation and will have no awareness that the activity of soul in which they are involved is the last link in a long chain that goes back to something that was started by this foundation in the middle of the twentieth century.

I close with a piece of verse that seems to me to capture what I have been trying to say. It is from the remarkable poem by W. H. Auden, "September 1, 1939," written at another dark moment in the history of the Western world. Here is the final stanza:

> Defenseless under the night
> Our world in stupor lies;
> Yet dotted everywhere,
> Ironic points of light
> Flash out wherever the Just
> Exchange their messages:
> May I, composed like them
> Of Eros, and of dust,
> Beleaguered by the same
> Negation and despair,
> Show an affirming flame.

For these twenty-five years of showing a brilliant and never-failing and affirming flame, our most serious and total appreciation, Mr. Leonard Read.

Index

This book was linotype set in the Times Roman series of type. The face was designed to be used in the news columns of the *London Times*. The *Times* was seeking a type face that would be condensed enough to accommodate a substantial number of words per column without sacrificing readability and still have an attractive, contemporary appearance. This design was an immediate success. It is used in many periodicals throughout the world and is one of the most popular text faces presently in use for book work.

Book design by Design Center, Inc., Indianapolis
Typography by Weimer Typesetting Co., Inc., Indianapolis
Printed by Hilltop Press Inc., Indianapolis